AN EXACT
REPLICA OF
A FIGMENT OF
MY IMAGINATION

AN EXACT
REPLICA OF
A FIGMENT OF
MY IMAGINATION

A MEMOIR

Elizabeth McCracken

Jonathan Cape
London

Published by Jonathan Cape 2009

2 4 6 8 10 9 7 5 3 1

First published in Great Britain in 2009 by
Jonathan Cape
Random House, 20 Vauxhall Bridge Road,
London SW1V 2SA

www.rbooks.co.uk

Addresses for companies within The Random House Group Limited can be found at:
www.randomhouse.co.uk/offices.htm

The Random House Group Limited Reg. No. 954009

A CIP catalogue record for this book is available from the British Library

ISBN 9780224087100

The Random House Group Limited supports The Forest Stewardship
Council (FSC), the leading international forest certification organisation.
All our titles that are printed on Greenpeace approved FSC certified paper
carry the FSC logo. Our paper procurement policy can be found at
www.rbooks.co.uk/environment

Mixed Sources
Product group from well-managed
forests and other controlled sources
www.fsc.org Cert no. TT-COC-2139
© 1996 Forest Stewardship Council
FSC

Printed and bound in Great Britain by
CPI Mackays, Chatham, Kent ME5 8TD

AN EXACT
REPLICA OF
A FIGMENT OF
MY IMAGINATION

O nce upon a time, before I knew anything about the subject, a woman told me that I should write a book about the lighter side of losing a child.

(This is not that book.)

I was giving a badly attended fiction reading at a public library in Florida. The woman wore enormous denim shorts, a plaid shirt, a black ponytail, and thumbprint-blurred glasses; her husband's nervous smile showed off his sand-colored teeth. They latched on to me, the way the sad and aimless sometimes do: I haven't been a public librarian myself for more than ten years now, but I retain what I like to think of as an air of civic acceptance. When the reading was over and the rest of the audience had dispersed (if five people can be said to disperse) she gave her suggestion. She really did say it, in a voice that seemed as thumbworn as her glasses: "You should write a book about the lighter side of losing a child. You're very funny."

I couldn't imagine what she was getting at. A joke book

for the bereaved? A comic strip guide to outliving your children?

For instance, she explained, her son was dead. Just recently she and Al — her husband, who smiled apologetically with those appalling choppers — had been on the beach, and Al had been eating a tuna sub, and a seagull came and stole part of the sandwich. And so she knew that the bird was the soul of her teenage son. Al nodded in agreement.

"And I laughed and laughed," the woman said flatly. I was sitting at a table, having signed three books, one for a cheerful old lady who'd called my short stories pointless during the Q & A. Al's wife had taken my place at the podium. She looked out at the empty chairs. "You should write a book with stories like that," she said. "It would be a big hit."

She was a childish, unnerving person. I imagined that she'd been trying people's patience for some time. At first they would have been sympathetic, but after her son had been dead for a while, they'd grow weary of her bringing him up as though the calamity had just happened. Well-meaning friends would look uncomfortable at the very mention of his name. So she had to devise new and sneaky ways to work him into conversations with strangers, at book readings, at the grocery store, at train station information desks, to telemarketers. *You have to move on,* beige-toothed Al might have said, *you can't mourn forever.* Then she could say, *See? I'm not mourning: I'm laughing. I'm look-ing on the lighter side.*

And now she wanted an instruction book.

It seemed like the saddest thing I'd ever heard, back be-fore I knew how sad things could get.

A child dies in this book: a baby. A baby is still-born. You don't have to tell me how sad that is: it happened to me and my husband, our baby, a son.

Still, I'm coming around to understanding what that woman in Florida wanted.

A baby is born in this book, too. That is to say, a healthy baby, our second child. The first child died on April 27, 2006, in France. The second baby — a biological fact lying across my lap asleep at this very moment as I type one-handed — was born one year and five days later in Saratoga Springs, New York. Not a miracle, I insist on it. Isn't that the headline in women's magazines, about stories like ours? "Our Miracle Baby"? I wouldn't have used the word *miracle* even before fate and biology and the law of averages kicked us in the teeth, back when I believed in luck, when I was a wisher on stars and white horses and pennies dropped in fountains. Those were the pastimes of my first pregnancy. This dozing infant is no miracle, though more than we had the nerve to hope for, a nice everyday baby, snoring now, the best possible thing: dreamt of, fretted over, even prayed for. A ginger-haired baby who conducts symphonies while sleeping, sighing at the dream music. (Those hands! They underscore closing arguments in dream-baby court; they hail dream-baby taxis.) We ourselves didn't pray (our religion is worry; we performed decades of it), but some of our friends did, and the mothers of friends, and nuns on two continents, our nuns-in-law. Such a beautiful, funny-looking, monkeyish, longed-for baby, exactly who we wanted to meet.

Every day as I love this baby in my lap, I think of my other baby. Poor older brother, poor missing one. I see the infant before me, the glory of the soles of the feet, the lips fattened and glossy with nursing, the nose whose future Edward and I try to predict daily. The love for the first magnifies the love for the second, and vice versa.

Now what I think that woman in Florida meant is: lighter things will happen to you, birds will steal your husband's sandwich on the beach, and your child will still be dead, and your husband's shock will still be funny, and you will spend your life trying to resolve this.

As for me, I believe that if there's a God — and I am as neutral on the subject as is possible — then the most basic proof of His existence is black humor. What else explains it, that odd, reliable comfort that billows up at the worst moments, like a beautiful sunset woven out of the smoke over a bombed city.

For instance: in the hospital in Bordeaux one of the midwives looked at us and asked a question in French. Most of the calamity (that word again; I can't come up with a better one) happened in French, which both Edward and I spoke only passably. Used to. My ability to speak French is gone, removed by the blunt-force trauma of those days. I've retained only occasional drifting words. Mostly I have to look things up. The French word for "midwife" is *sage-femme,* wise woman, I remember that. This particular wise woman was a teenager, checking items off a list. The room was like a hospital room anywhere, on a ward for the reproductively luckless, far away from babies and their exhausted mothers. Did we want to speak to—

"Excusez-moi?" Edward said, and cocked an ear.

"Une femme religieuse," the midwife clarified. A religious woman. Ah.

Here's what she said:

Voulez-vous parler à une nonne?

Which means, Would you like to speak to a nun? More nuns: of course in Catholic France, it was assumed that we were Catholic.

But Edward heard:

Voulez-vous parler à un nain?

Which means, Would you like to speak to a dwarf?

When he told this to his friend Claudia, she said, "My God! You must have thought, That's the last thing I need!"

"No," Edward told her. "I thought I'd really like to speak to a dwarf about then. I thought it might cheer me up."

We theorized that every French hospital kept a supply of dwarfs in the basement for the worst-off patients and their families. Or maybe it was just a Bordelaise tradition: the dwarfs of grief. We could see them in their apologetic smallness, shifting from foot to foot.

In the days afterward, I told this story to friends over the phone. We were still in Bordeaux. The hospital had wanted to keep me, but Edward explained that we would check into a nearby hotel—we lived an hour away in an old farmhouse—and come back for the follow-up examination. It will be better for our morale, he said in French, and the doctor nodded. Our terrible news had been relayed by my friends Wendy and Ann to the rest of my friends in America, and now I phoned to say—to say what, I wasn't sure, but I didn't want to disappear into France and grief. I called on our cell phone from our hotel room or from sidewalk cafés in the woundingly lovely French spring. Everything hurt. We ordered carafe after carafe of rosé, and I told my friends about the Dwarfs of Grief, and I listened to their loud, shocked, relieved laughter. I felt a strange responsibility to sound as though I were not going mad with sorrow. Maybe I managed it. At that moment I felt so ruined by life that I couldn't imagine it ever getting worse, which just shows that my sense of humor was slightly more durable than my imagination.

Edward and I made a lot of plans that week; we thought all sorts of things were possible. For instance, we decided as we wept that we would go somewhere we'd never been as soon as we could. We were leaving France anyhow: we'd been there for a year and a half, and I'd landed a teaching job in the United States in the fall. Edward would look after the baby while I was at school. Our plan had been to go straight to the States, to Saratoga Springs, to settle in before my job started in September. Instead, we decided to pack the house and just—go. Barcelona, maybe. We pictured ourselves walking beneath a hot, unfamiliar sun, somewhere where the drinks were plentiful and not made in France. We believed that a short while devoted to oblivion and beauty would make us feel better. We thought that we *could* feel better. Soon enough the notion seemed ludicrous, and we forgot about our Spanish plans. Instead we spent the summer in England, on the North Norfolk coast, looking at the North Sea and hoping that Edward's U.S. immigration application would be straightened out by fall.

Maybe Spain was just like my early jokes: I wanted to say something to my friends and family that wasn't *Our child died and our life is over.*

Anyhow, for a few days we were stuck in Bordeaux, killing time until my follow-up appointment. I didn't want to eat, we couldn't drink forever, the hotel room was claustrophobic. Our second morning, we decided to walk through a flea market in a nearby park just to look at something different. All spring we'd gone to French flea markets, driving hours to look at piles of junk, or preposterously priced Louis XVI armoires, or glorious 1930s French bookends. Over the months we'd bought a handsome old clock and a sign advertising oysters, a pair of vases made of WWII artillery shells and a lampshade hand-painted with sea serpents of the here-be-dragons variety. We'd even been to this very flea market the week before, after an appointment with an anesthesiologist.

(He wanted to look at my back to see if I was a good candidate for an epidural, should I need one; he'd said in English, while thumbing my spine, "You see, I may come across your back in the middle of the night. You say you aren't going to show up in the middle of the night, but somehow you always do. Three, four in the morning, there you are. Always I see you in the middle of the night."

"I'll try my best to avoid it," I said. I planned on avoiding an epidural altogether.

He said, gravely, "Even so.")

At the Bordeaux flea market a week later we started down the aisles between vendor tents. Every step I took made me sick. All those flea markets we'd gone to were just a form of daydreaming: we were buying objects for some future house we'd live in with the nice baby we were going to have. The glass light-up globe would go on his bookshelf. The low chair upholstered in old carpet would be perfect for nursing. In the spring we would flea-market as a family, the baby in his sling cuddled up while I leaned over one of those flat cases filled with metal whatnots, jewelry, cutlery, old coins, one hand on his head to protect him, the other pointing, as I said, "Excusez-moi, madame . . ."

You see, I'd thought he was a sure thing.

Now we passed uncomfortable-looking striped sofas, beat-up leather club chairs, birdcages, chipped teacups, immaculate teacups, the heirless heirlooms of anonymous French people: a kind of fossil record. Vendors with their lunches of wine and bread and oysters balanced plates on their knees. We waded in farther, and I started to gasp.

"We're going," said Edward, taking my weight against him, leading me out. "We're going, we're going. We're going, sweetheart, this way."

If he hadn't been next to me, I think I would have fallen to the ground and stayed there.

And *that,* soon enough, was how I felt all of the time.

Where are they when we need them, the Dwarfs of Grief, we sometimes said to each other, when things were really bad.

Which is to say:

I want it, too, the impossible lighter-side book. I will always be a woman whose first child died, and I won't give up either that grievance or the bad jokes of everyday life. I will hold on to both forever. I want a book that acknowledges that life goes on but that death goes on, too, that a person who is dead is a long, long story. You move on from it, but the death will never disappear from view. Your friends may say, *Time heals all wounds.* No, it doesn't, but eventually you'll feel better. You'll be yourself again. Your child will still be dead. The frivolous parts of your personality, stubborner than you'd imagined, will grow up through the cracks in your soul. The sad lady at the Florida library meant: the lighter side is not that your child has died — no lighter side to that — but that the child lived and died in this human realm, with its breathtaking sadness and dumb punch lines and hungry seagulls. That was the good news. She wasn't going to pretend that he hadn't, no matter how the mention of him made people shift and look away.

A stillborn child is really only ever his death. He didn't live: that's how he's defined. Once he fades from memory, there's little evidence at all, nothing that could turn up, for instance, at a French flea market, or be handed down through the family. Eventually we are all only our artifacts. I am writing this before our first child turns into the set of footprints the French midwives made for us at the hospital, the stack of condolence cards that tracked us down as we fled France — things that our descendants, whoever they are, however many, might stumble across and wonder about. The urn for his ashes we burned; the ashes we scattered; the hospital bills we paid off. The midwives asked us if we wanted his picture taken. I'd seen nineteenth-century photos, dark with age and fingerprints, children unasleep with eyes closed, maybe a toy wedged in a hand, you could see what was wrong, in the neck, in the mouth: everything. More fossils for the flea market. A dead orphaned child now floating down generations of strangers. Those morbid Victorians, I thought, back when I believed that stillbirth was a Victorian problem. But now I considered the midwives' offer. This was my child, and surely —

It was Edward who said, decisively, no, because he was afraid we'd make a fetish of it, and he was right. The photo would not have been of our child, just his body. Only from this distance do I understand the difference.

I imagine those descendants, direct or indirect, cousins

many times removed, the greatest of nephews and nieces (one of the ways in which I've changed forever is that even half joking I will not say *grandchildren* despite this here snoring baby), someone dear and distant, saying, *Their first child was stillborn.* But how will they have heard? Will we sit down and tell our second child and maybe, here's hoping, our third, about their older brother, or will we leave them to find out for themselves?

I don't want those footprints framed on the wall, but I don't want to hide them beneath the false bottom of a trunk. I don't want to wear my heart on my sleeve or put it away in cold storage. I don't want to fetishize, I don't want to repress, I want his death to be what it is: a fact. Something that people know without me having to explain it. I don't feel the need to tell my story to everyone, but when people ask, *Is this your first child?* I can't bear any of the possible answers.

I'm not ready for my first child to fade into history.

*T*his is the happiest story in the world with the saddest ending.

That's the sentence that kept threading through my brain in Bordeaux. I wrote it down in a notebook; otherwise I would have forgotten.

We lived an hour away from the city and that grim hospital, in an enormous rented farmhouse with a converted attached barn, an oddball structure called Savary, which had at one point been a home for single mothers and their troubled children. The house had eight bedrooms and as many bathrooms and a vast haunted space upstairs that the landlady referred to as the Dormitory, which smelled of disemboweled teddy bears and tear-stained twin mattresses. Downstairs, in the old-barn part of the house, sofas were backed up against old cattle-feed troughs. Savary was a certain species of French house, the preposterous property bought by an English person dreaming of *les bonheurs* and high summer rents; we paid almost nothing for October through May, when it would have stood empty anyhow. Everything came from Ikea: sheets, drinking glasses, light fixtures, beds, kitchen appliances. The walls were stone, and the floors cold tile.

In my memory the house is gothic, all corridors and abandoned bedrooms. My office was upstairs, off what was described in the inventory as the Second Lounge but really was a space too lumpen to be a hallway and too windowless and eave-cramped to be a room. Getting to my office after dark involved crossing a series of spaces whose light switches were right where I didn't need them. I almost never went. Instead, I stayed by the fire in the front room. We decided we would be hardy: we left the furnace off to save money and wrote, Cratchit-like, in hats and gloves. The place was full of mice. I could even hear them skittering underneath the tub when I bathed. Sometimes we heard a worse noise: according to Maud, the young Irishwoman hired to look after the property, there was a pine marten living in the eaves. I didn't even know what a pine marten was, but in my gloves and hat I imagined a raccoonish, foxish Jacob Marley, rattling his chains above our bedroom to make us feel fully Dickensian. I hated that animal, though I never saw it.

In fact, from where I sit now — New York State, the spring of 2007 — everything about our winter in Savary feels dire: the house dirty, the Anglophone friends we made perpetually and depressingly drunk and broke, the language barrier alienating. A single sentence in French can make me sad. Every now and then I will suddenly think, What was the name of the next village over, the one with the covered market in the middle, what was the name of that restaurant we used to go to, and I find I can't remember, the information's gone like a pulled tooth, though my brain will keep poking at the empty spot.

What a terrible time that all was, I'll think.

My memory is a goddamn liar. It can only see France — or at least those seven months in the southwestern countryside — through the calamity. If you'd asked before April 27, 2006, I would have said: *This is the happiest time of my life.* That's why I wrote down that sentence in the hospital, *This is the happiest story in the world with the saddest ending.* It was very strange to have been so happy so recently, and I felt that if I puzzled it over enough I might be able to find my way back — not to experience it again, of course, but to conjure up the smell on the hem of an article of clothing, to touch in some abstract way something that had innocently, casually touched my happiness, since there would be (he was stillborn) nothing literal for me to touch.

But now there it is when I wipe the smudge away: happiness. I was two months pregnant when we moved to Savary. We'd spent the nine months before that in Paris. For three years we'd split our time between Iowa, where we taught and earned money, and Europe, where we wrote and spent it: Paris twice, Ireland, Berlin, Denmark. People told me, "I'd love to have your life," and I would always say,

"But then you'd have to accept my standard of living." We didn't own a house, a car, not even a sofa. We spent our money on souvenir busts and cheap red wine.

Savary was one more adventure. Yes, the house was dark, but it was agreeably hilarious. "We're living in an unwed mothers' home," I told my friends. "We have eight bathrooms and two kitchens and a single possible pine marten." The house was surrounded by farmland and vineyards, cows out some windows and horses out others, and a vast patio off the summer kitchen with a view of Duras, the nearby village, and its medieval hill-set château. The château was an enormous plain castle that looked, in good weather, like the home of seven beautiful princesses and one befuddled king, and in bad weather like the keep of a brooding, evil, terribly attractive beast.

I loved being pregnant. Whatever hormones had shaken together in my bloodstream, it was an agreeable cocktail. I devoted myself to gestating—I didn't write much, but that didn't bother me. Edward cooked and cleaned and tucked me into bed. I rubbed my stomach and loved my husband profoundly. I had the sense that these last months as a twosome were as important as our upcoming months as a threesome: they felt like part of someone's happy childhood. What fun it would be to tell our kid where his parents had spent his gestation and birth. In the spring, sheep and lambs, cows and calves, studded the hills, and I regarded them. I felt stupidly, sentimentally mammalian.

After the baby died, I told Edward over and over again that I didn't want to forget any of it: the happiness was real, as real as the baby himself, and it would be terrible, unforgivable, to forget it. His entire life had turned out to be the forty-one weeks and one day of his gestation, and those days were happy. We couldn't pretend that they weren't. It would be like pretending that he himself was a bad thing, something to be regretted, and I didn't. I would have done the whole thing over again even knowing how it would end.

(Would I really? It's a kind of maternal puzzle I can't get at even now: he isn't here, and yet how can I even consider wishing him away? I can't love and regret him both. He isn't here, but now someone else is, this thrilling splendiferous second baby, and like any mother I can't imagine taking the smallest step from the historical path that led me here, to this one, to such a one.)

No matter how I vowed to hold on to the happiness of the pregnancy, it was impossible, such a solitary pastime. When your child dies you cannot talk about how much you loved being pregnant. You have to give up the stories about the funny French gym you went to, where the women kissed hello while on treadmills and the gym owner shook your hand and said, "Ça va? Et le bébé?" You must retire the anecdotes of meeting a pair of Mormons in Bergerac, the comic complaints of how impossible it is for a pregnant person to eat in a French restaurant, your run-ins with

French lab workers who refused — pen poised over a cup of your urine, one eyebrow raised skeptically — to believe there was such a thing as a married woman who kept her maiden name. You can't list all the funny names you and your husband came up with for the kid, laughing in bed, late at night. You will lose nine months of your history along with all the other things you've lost.

I had just stepped over the border from happy pregnancy to grief, but I could still see that better, blither country, could smell the air over my shoulder, could remember my fluency there, the dumb jokes, the gestures, the disappointing cuisine, the rarefied climate. I knew already I could never go back, not then, not for any future pregnancy (should I be so lucky).

Of course I wanted to remember what it was like! It was all I had.

Now it's all miles away. Everything's muddled together. At some point I imagined a kind of time — I don't know whether I got this idea from science or science fiction, not being much interested in either — that split into two or more directions when the baby died: on one track he lived and we took him home and somewhere in the universe at this moment we have a one-year-old baby and a newborn and are ignorant, exhausted, cheery (or maybe only the first two); on the other track, the one I accidentally took, he died, and we left France. But time changed backwards, too, and now, no matter what, every single day of my first pregnancy, when I was laughing till I was paralytic at my own jokes about what to name the baby, when I was addressing fond monologues to my stomach as I drove a horrific old Ford Escort through the French countryside, he was already dead, and France was already culpable, and our hearts were already broken.

If you'd asked me five years ago — let's say five years ago and seven weeks — where I saw myself, five years and seven weeks in the future, I would not have mentioned a husband, children, living in six different countries. I was thirty-five and had never had a really serious romance. This mostly didn't bother me. I liked living alone. I even liked going to movies alone and eating in restaurants alone. I would never have called myself single. The word suggests a certain willingness to flirt in bars or take out advertisements for oneself on the Internet: single people are social in the hope that they won't be single forever. I was a spinster, a woman no one imagined marrying. That suited me. I would be the weird aunt, the oddball friend who bought the great presents and occasionally drank too much and fell asleep on the sofa. Actually, I already *was* that person.

Then I went to a party in New York thrown by Barnes and Noble and discovered that the author of that weird illustrated book I'd liked so much was not, as I'd concluded from the work and author photo, a midforties, balding, puffy misanthrope, but a cheerful, floppy-haired thirtyish Englishman. A month later, he came to Boston to work on an art project and called me up. We went out every night for a week. On our third date, he said, "I have something to tell you." It transpired that his name was not, as was printed on his book, Edward Carey, but in fact, as was printed on his passport, Jonathan Edward Carey Harvey. He displayed the passport to prove this. As revelations went, I could live with it, though it was too late for me to call him anything but Edward. At the end of the week, on our fifth date — which happened to be his thirty-second birthday — he asked me very seriously if I wanted children.

The only other people who'd asked me that question were my similarly aging childless girlfriends. The answer I generally gave was: not abstractly, but if I met someone who really wanted children, and I thought he'd be a good father, and I was relatively sure we'd be married forever or at least for the length of two roughly concurrent childhoods, then yes, I would want children, yes please. I loved family life, adored my parents and my older brother, our decades-old running jokes, our familial obsessions. We went out for long, boozy meals. We took trips together and brought home souvenirs and outlandish stories. The McCracken Family Circus. We even went to the actual circus together, all four of us being actual circus buffs. Yes: I would want children if I met someone with whom I could imagine raising eccentric, friendly, hilarious children who we could bundle off to Europe and museums and circuses no matter how old or young they were. At thirty-five it seemed unlikely I'd meet such a person. That was OK. If life never brought me a husband or children, I wouldn't miss them. I'd devote myself to good works or bad habits.

But I could tell that Edward wasn't asking idly. He has a wide forehead upon which all emotions are legible: sincerity, anxiety, apprehension, skepticism; he has passed it down to our sincere, apprehensive, occasionally skeptical second baby. My answer would make a difference.

"Yes," I said. "I think I would."

A week after that—it has been five years and seven weeks, Mother, and I no longer feel the need to juggle the ledgers—he moved into my apartment. When people ask where we met, I sometimes say, "I ordered him from Barnes and Noble."

I'd lived for nine years in Somerville, Massachusetts: now Edward and I began to move. For four years, we relocated every few months, to Iowa City, Paris, Ireland, Iowa City, Berlin, small-town Denmark, Iowa City, Paris. We chased jobs and fellowships and wine and museums, lived in midwestern sabbatical sublets, a thatched cottage that had sheltered Brecht in the 1930s, next door to hard-partying students, in a German villa made over into housing for American academics. Somewhere in there we got married at the small stone church at the bottom of Edward's parents' driveway. The village vicar officiated, backed up by an American rabbi my mother had ordered off the Internet.

My favorite of our dwellings was our last apartment in Paris, the first home of my first pregnancy. We'd had a list of things we wanted in a place to live: space for two desks, maybe a guest room, maybe a tiny balcony, without a doubt an elevator for certain unsteady relatives. Then we answered an ad in an expat paper. The building was next to the Jewish Museum and around the corner from the Pompidou Centre. We punched the code we'd been given over the phone into the pad by the door, walked five flights of stairs that got narrower and wobblier until we were at the top in a low-ceilinged hallway, rang a bell, and were let into a seventeenth-century high-ceilinged cartoon garret filled with antique furniture. It fulfilled none of our requirements. We loved it immediately. Just then another would-be renter showed up, a yellow-clad lawyer from Boston, with wooden skin and leaden hair and the official dreary insinuating underfed brittle aura of a number 2 pencil. We understood that she meant us ill. "We'll take it," Edward told the landlady, a tall woman from Amiens who raised mules and taught English to small boys. "Wonderful," the landlady answered, and the lawyer said in disbelief, "It's fine for *one* person. But two?"

"We're writers," I said apologetically. "We're supposed to live in a garret in Paris."

She snorted. "*Everyone* in Paris is a writer."

The kitchen was small and overlooked the dining area; the guest room was a treacherous loft over the living room; the tub was a slipper bath, half-sized but deep, with a step to sit on, the perfect place to read. Above the bed, where I worked, sitting up, was a ceiling of herringbone beams. Through the bedroom window you could see the turrets of the National Archives; through the dining room window, the chimney pots of Paris.

I was working on a malingering novel, since abandoned (for a while I said, "It died," but not anymore), and Edward on an enormous one. We'd write in the morning, Edward in the dining room and me propped up in bed, and then I'd persuade him to go out to lunch, where we'd order a carafe of wine, and then we'd wander and spend money and not get back to our books till the next morning.

After some months of this, my novel collapsed. I panicked: How would I ever write again? How could we afford to keep living in Paris at this rate? To talk me down from the cliff, Edward suggested the country, where life would be beautiful, cheap, and dull, and we'd have no choice but to work. All right, I said. We found three possible properties on the Internet; we drove out to look at them. The first was a millhouse that had been converted into a restaurant and was now being converted back into a house; from the windows we could see the landlord's apartment, which seemed overly cozy. The second, also a millhouse, had an intermittent rat problem. "Coypou," the landlady explained, and Edward said, "Oh, coypou," as though this constituted a particularly prestigious sort of rat problem. The third was Savary. Beryl, the landlady, showed us around. Preposterous! we thought. Who needed four times as many toilets as occupants? But the price was right, and we signed a lease that started in three months, and we went back to Paris.

Two weeks later, I sent Edward out to negotiate a pregnancy test. All slightly medical transactions in French pharmacies require negotiation with the pharmacist. I took it, disbelieved it, sent him out for another, which agreed with the first.

W e didn't call my occupant the Baby, which seemed inaccurate, cloying, and too optimistic. We were superstitious. For some complicated, funny-only-to-the-progenitors reason, we settled on the names Pudding and Wen (in case we were having twins, which, as the daughter of a twin, I worried about). Then the first ultrasound showed the single pocket-watch heart, and so it was just Pudding, boy or girl. What's Pudding doing? How are you, Pudding? The baby ticking away was Pudding all September in Paris, and Pudding when we moved to the countryside in October. And then we had the amnio, and Pudding seemed to suit a little boy, the little boy we were making up day by day — I made him up literally, of course, cell by cell and gram by gram, and Edward and I made him up in conversation and dumb flights of fancy. Pudding! we'd say to my stomach. Pudding, what are you up to? Pudding was Pudding to us and soon enough to all our friends and family: everyone called him that. I couldn't imagine naming a baby ahead of time, calling a baby by his earth name before he was a citizen of this world. Naming seemed a kind of passport stamp.

But it was one of the first things we were told, after we found out that he was dead: the baby needed a name. I was sitting outside the first hospital of the day, waiting with Sylvie, the midwife who we'd found to deliver the baby. She was a sinewy woman in her midforties who spoke about ten words of English but was hugely enthusiastic. We'd just heard the bad news. I was more than forty-one weeks pregnant. It was late April and the weather was fine and it was better not to be inside any kind of medical room for the moment. Sylvie was holding my hand. Soon we'd go to a different hospital. This hospital was only for living children. They didn't do autopsies. We needed an autopsy. Sylvie and I sat across from two teenage boys who were smoking, and more than anything I wanted to ask one for a cigarette but I didn't.

The language of disaster is, handily, the language of the barely fluent. I kept saying to Sylvie, *Je ne comprends pas. C'est incroyable. C'est incroyable.* Edward was at the far end of the parking lot, calling his parents on our cell phone since we'd come to one of those moments of nothing to do.

You must find a name, Sylvie said. For the certificate.

How could we pick a name out of the handful we'd idly considered? How could we do that to him? Oh, I don't mean to be maudlin, and I do not believe in some lousy afterlife where babies who don't get to be born are ushered off by a kindly black-and-white angel, a real creepy Boy Scout leader of an angel. I hate that fucking angel, cupping the downy heads of all those unborn babies, almost as much as I hate the phrase "unborn baby" itself, I am trying to disbelieve him so I don't have to look at him, but he's lodged in my head. He's rounding them up, he's saying, *Come here, little souls, it's not your time yet — tell me your name — what did your parents call you?*

No more talk of angels. I can't stand the tendency to speak of dead children as such. I do not want him elevated to angel. I do not want him demoted to neverness. He was a person, that's all.

Edward came back from the privacy of the far reaches of the parking lot, still holding the cell phone. He wasn't crying anymore, but he had been. I told him we had to name the baby for legal reasons.

"We'll call him Pudding," he said, in one of those moments that sounds improbably sentimental to me now but at that moment was exactly right. A new name would be only a death name, another way to say that he hadn't exactly existed before now. How could he suddenly be an Oscar or a Moses? How would he ever find his way, renamed like that? His parents called him Pudding, always. Even now we do. It's the name on the certificate the city of Bordeaux gave us in early May, *certificat d'enfant sans vie,* certificate of the birth of a child without life — birth certificate, death certificate, whatever you want to call it. Sometimes it seems too sweet to me, but mostly I just think: that's who he is, he's Pudding.

I'm glad we were in a foreign country. The French probably thought it was an ordinary Anglo-Saxon name, like William, or Randolph, or George.

From the time I was a child and learned what *first person singular* meant, I found even the phrase itself beautiful. Most of my life, from childhood to spinsterhood, I had no pronoun problems. Partnered women with their confusing plurals turned my stomach. Who cared whether you and your beloved liked a particular restaurant in unison? Who believed that it was even possible? The love letters I intended to write would be first person and second person: I, you, never we. Even once I met and married Edward, I did my best to avoid the insidious *we,* which suggested we were a two-bodied, one-brained science-fiction creature, a mutant born of romance. And yet here I am, writing a book as a love letter to Edward and trying to explain — well, every time I try to get further than this into a sentence about Edward, I end up flummoxed: he was so loving and grief-stricken and so careful to set aside his pain to take care of me, and everything I write seems inadequate and sickeningly sweet. Even that last sentence feels inadequate and sick-eningly sweet. We went through everything together, and writing *we* feels presumptuous, because he can speak for himself, and writing *I* feels presumptuous, because the calamity happened to both of us, was just as awful for both of us.

Ah, we. When I was pregnant both times and people re-ferred to me and Edward as *the three of you* or me as *the two of you,* it always felt wrong. Three of us was the goal, and eventually the mostly foregone conclusion both times. But any photograph would clearly show: there were still only two of us. For the rest of my life, I think, plurals will con-fuse me. How many children do I have? How many are there of me?

I'm lying when I say I didn't get much writing done when I was pregnant with Pudding. True enough for a while. Most days I woke up and had breakfast and then took another nap and then watched some television. Savary had English satellite TV, and I became addicted to the gentle afternoon reality programs of the BBC, all auctions and car boot sales. The two sofas in the main living room weren't very comfortable, but they were deep and difficult to get out of, or so I told myself.

But when I was about eight months pregnant, I did something I'd never imagined doing: I started a memoir. Not only a memoir, but one in which I appeared frequently with my pants off. A memoir that would include the phrase *my cervix*, meaning mine, Elizabeth McCracken's. What the hell: I couldn't bend my attention to writing anything else, and I was eight months pregnant, past the danger point, so I thought, so I thought, and I began a funny book about being pregnant in France. I didn't tell anyone except Edward and my friend Ann, because, of course: bad luck.

My great-grandfather believed in the evil eye. When registering his eleven children at school (according to his daughter, my grandmother), he would never say how many there were. When you got cocky and kept count, the evil eye could snatch away a child. This was the same reason we never decided for sure on a name, the same reason Edward and I never, not once, talked about our future with our baby without looking for a piece of wood to touch. When the pregnancy was brand-new, in Paris, we became such devoted knockers of wood that we had a hard time making any progress through the city, lurching as we did toward park benches, paneled storefronts, tree stakes, and actual trees. We would have knocked on *anything*. It's amazing we didn't fling ourselves into department stores, asking desperate directions to the furniture department, please, *monsieur*, quick to a bedpost, as we wondered what the wood-knocking statute of limitations was, after you had said aloud something that required it. Later Edward admitted to me that when he was alone in Bergerac, he went into the church and lit candles for Pudding's safe arrival. He put his hand on his wooden bedside table so often that he was surprised it didn't take on the shape of a loose glove from erosion, like a stone he'd seen in Santiago de Compostela that has been touched by centuries of pilgrims.

Pregnant with Pudding, I didn't buy baby clothes, told my family not to buy baby clothes. And then, when I was six months pregnant, I broke down. My first purchase was two pairs of tiny baby shoes in Bergerac: a pair of loafers and some light blue leather boots with mod spaceships flying across the toes.

"I thought you weren't going to buy anything," Edward said.

"These are not for Pudding," I said. "They're for some other little boy."

And with that it was easy to start buying clothing, and easy to start a memoir all about my happy, uneventful pregnancy. Easy to thumb my nose at the evil eye. We knocked on wood and made wishes, but by eight months all the wishes I made were like a smug joke I had with myself. I knocked wood and I wished on stars, but sometimes there was something else to wish for, something that hadn't already been taken care of, and so I did.

I just thought he was a sure thing.

I wrote about our doctors, my search for a gym in the French countryside, what we ate, our friends down the road. It would make a good book, I thought: I'd end it with the three of us leaving France together. I tried not to write sentences that made it sound as though he were already born and things were fine, because I wasn't willing to tempt the evil eye *that* much. Eventually I wrote 170 pages. They're still somewhere on my computer.

That's another reason I wrote down, *This is the happiest*

story in the world with the saddest ending: I was in the habit of narrating my daily life.

I didn't write a single word of this second book during my second pregnancy.

H ere's what else we didn't do when I was pregnant the second time.

Knock wood. Light candles. Tell ninety percent of the people we knew that I was pregnant. Have an amniocentesis. Pick up pennies. Wish on: stars, white horses, alarm clocks reading 11:11, wishbones, blown dandelion fluff. Buy baby clothes. Pick names. Find out the baby's gender. Come up with an in utero name: the kid was "the kid" or "whoever it is" or merely the unspoken result of "if everything goes right." Begin sentences, "After the baby's born . . ." Toss spilled salt over left shoulders. Give a fuck about the number thirteen no matter where it showed up.

No matter how much we wanted to.

I can't remember how long we'd known that Pudding was dead before we declared that we would have another child, or which one of us first said it. Certainly it was within minutes of hearing the bad news, and we both kept repeating it, not because we were done with this baby, but because that sentence — we'll have another child, we'll have another child — was like throwing out a towline. It was like believing in the future instead of in the place we were at that moment. We vowed to try as soon as possible.

"But not in August," I said after a while. August was when Pudding was conceived. August meant an April or May baby. That seemed like too much.

And then we left France, and I decided to be practical about everything. I was thirty-nine, I wasn't going to toss away a whole month like that. Anyhow, what were the chances? How could we count on anything?

So I couldn't say, We *will* have another child. Instead, I said, "I *hope* we can have another child." It was bad enough grieving for this child, my Pudding, without lamenting other only theoretical children. I missed the child we lost and I wanted another and these seemed like two absolutely separate aches.

He was a person. I missed him like a person. Seeing babies on the street did not stab me with pain the way I know they stab some grieving women, those who have lost children or simply desperately want to have them. For me, other babies were other babies. They weren't who I was missing. Every now and then a baby could take me by surprise and make me weep — for instance, an e-mailed photo of my cousin Rosalie's son, who (I realized as I stared at it, and closed the file, and opened it up again) looked like I'd imagined Pudding, though as it happened we shared none of the same blood. Babies born to mothers who'd been pregnant at the same time as me hurt a little. I didn't mind hearing about them, but I didn't want to meet them. That puzzled me since it wasn't logical, and even in mourning I liked to think I was logical, but it was an unhappiness that rose up in me, even months later when I was already pregnant though not broadcasting it, and I saw a friend who'd had a baby three months after me, a wonderful woman who—because she had just become a mother—was so sympathetic and sweet to me. Most people didn't even mention Pudding; she enfolded me in a hug and said, "Oh, Elizabeth, I am so sorry about your baby"—and I just wanted her to *leave,* because I didn't want to be a good and decent and functioning human being and ask after *her* baby. Even now I have a hard time with the babies born to friends around Pudding's birth. It's not logical, and yet there it is: this one is one month older, this one three weeks younger.

But mostly I just missed my own child.

About a week after Pudding's death I got in my e-mail box a photograph of the newborn son of a very lovely woman who'd been a student of mine at Iowa. She'd known I was pregnant, but her friends had very wisely kept silent about what had happened, so as not to terrify her, and therefore her husband didn't know he shouldn't send me a photograph of a newborn baby boy. A few weeks later, and it would have been fine: by then, when friends reported that someone I knew had had a baby, they usually added, "I didn't know whether to tell you or not, but I figure . . ."

"Oh," I always said, "if human reproduction has to carry on, I want it to work out for people I like."

Still, I wouldn't have minded a pause in the whole business. A sudden harmless moratorium on babies being born. Doctors would have to tell the unfortunate pregnant, "I'm sorry. It happens sometimes. Tidal, we think. For everyone else, nine months, but for you, eleven months, maybe a year, maybe more. Don't go outside. Don't leave your house. Stroke your stomach, fine, but only in your own living room. Keep your lullabies to yourself. We'll let you know when it's time."

That lovely former student sent a horrified apology when she found out what had happened, but of course I understood. That is one of the strangest side effects of the whole story. I am that thing worse than a cautionary tale: I am a horror story, an example of something terrible going wrong when you least expect it, and for no good reason, a story to be kept from pregnant women, a story so grim and lesson-less it's better not to think about at all.

Where in France did we live? In the middle of the southwest of the country. In an area called Aquitaine. In a department called Lot-et-Garonne. Forty-five minutes southwest of Cyrano's Bergerac. Forty minutes east of the tower where Montaigne wrote for the last years of his life. Our address was in the village of Baleyssagues, but the closest place to buy bread and wine and cheese was Duras: three bakeries, a post office, two bars, two pharmacies; Marguerite Duras took her pen name from the town, which is where her father was buried (though not where her own first child, a son, was stillborn in 1942). The nearest train station was in Sainte Foy la Grand. We were, of course, an hour east of Bordeaux.

My friend Lib has a French friend who lives in Cambridge, Massachusetts, who lost a baby to sudden infant death syndrome. When she found out about Pudding, she said, sadly, "Now France will be ruined for them." America had been ruined for her, but that loss meant nothing compared to the loss of her daughter. But to lose France, as she knew we would, to lose both France and a child —

It's a part of the world I will never, ever, ever go back to.

Pregnant with Pudding, I wanted things simple, easy, low intervention. (For my second child I would have agreed to anything, a simultaneous caesarean/induction/being-pounded-on-the-back-like-a-ketchup-bottle/forceps/extra-drugs/extra-pain delivery.) My first obstetrician was a blond woman from Baltimore who practiced at the upscale American Hospital of Paris. I chose her after looking at the hospital Web site. I wanted a female doctor, and the only other choice was a very glamorous Frenchwoman whose photo seemed to have been taken at sunrise outside a disco.

Dr. Baltimore was a strange combination of businesslike practices and motherliness. She said to the dreamy waving image on the sonogram screen, "Hello, sweetheart!" But she could never quite look Edward in the eye. She was extremely smart and certain, and I found her smarts and certainty calming. On the other hand, every time we tried to explain that we were moving to the country, she came up with some vague plan in which it would be easy enough to come back to deliver in Paris. She did this so automatically and seamlessly — as though we'd *asked* for her to come up with a plan — that it was hypnotic. We never argued. "Right," she said at the first visit, fiddling with a small, round paper wheel that reminded me of a teenage girl's fortune-telling device. "Right. April 18. Well, you could just arrange to be back here for that month."

The second visit, when we explained that moving back would be expensive and uncertain, she suggested we could just sleep on a friend's sofa. The third time she said, well, I'd come in, and if everything looked all right, she could "help things along."

It wasn't till we'd left the office that I realized she'd meant induction. Oh no, I thought: Pudding's birthday was his decision, not mine. Indeed we did come back from the countryside for a few appointments, for the amnio, for the big four-month sonogram, but then we decided it was time to look for someone closer to Savary, whether or not Dr. Baltimore thought it was a good idea. We heard awful things about the nearest hospital, in Marmande, and so we crossed that off our list and looked at the other nearby medium-sized cities.

My second doctor was a short, comical Frenchman who spoke idiosyncratic English and practiced in Bergerac, forty minutes away from Savary. He was the only English speaker at the hospital. Dr. Bergerac was in his forties, with black hair that looked painted on and high color in his cheeks. Altogether he seemed like a European hand puppet of a doctor. We sat in his office—he'd decorated the walls with Tintin posters, which made us like him—and he fiddled with the fortune-telling wheel, and said, "OK. Twenty-seven Avril." This was how we learned that French pregnancies last longer than American pregnancies, at least officially.

Like Dr. Baltimore, Dr. Bergerac had a sonogram machine in his office, and on our first visit he gave me a routine ultrasound. "Il bouge!" said Dr. Bergerac. *He moves!* "You have had coffee today. You know what is the gender? Your last *échographie,* did he say?"

"I had an amnio," I said. "So we know it's a boy."

"Yes," he said. "I agree with this. It is a boy." He moved the cursor on the screen and typed next to the relevant lump: B O Y.

Afterward he had a midwife give us a tour of the charming maternity ward. True enough, if something went wrong we'd miss the American Hospital with all its bells and whistles and impeccably clean floors, but this place seemed cozy. A midwife walked down the hall, carrying a red baby with a full head of dark hair. I had never seen such a baby. The Bergerac hospital clearly did good work.

My next appointment was attended by a very cute blond intern, who Dr. Bergerac was clearly trying to impress. During the sonogram, he spoke to her in French, explaining that we were writers from England, *voilà,* the placenta, a lot of English people liked to come to this area of France, the Dordogne, there's the baby's head, the English found it inspiring, look, the bladder. Then he told her to check my cervix and left the room to talk to Edward. I lay back. The intern rummaged around in the manner of an unhappy wife looking for a wedding ring in a garbage disposal: dutifully, thoroughly, but without much sentiment.

Afterward the doctor asked me how tall I was.

"Not very," I joked.

"I suffer from this problem as well," he said. "But 'ow tall? Do not answer in feets, I do not understand them."

I shrugged. He gave me a flat-handed "please rise" gesture and appraised me.

"I am writing for you a prescription for pelvicscan," he said.

"Pardon?"

"A hex-ray," he explained.

At home I poked around on the Internet and asked doctor friends. As far as I could tell, there was no good reason for prenatal X-rays — they could really tell you nothing about how easy it would be to go through labor — and there seemed to be a slight risk of childhood leukemia associated with them. I e-mailed Dr. Bergerac to ask him if I could forgo it. He said no. Don't worry! It's not dangerous! But it is obligatory!

And so I just never went back.

(I've always thought I was five feet even, but at my six-week postpartum checkup, the nurse announced, much to my surprise, that I was five one. Which makes me 156 centimeters tall.)

Of course it occurs to me that Pudding might have lived if I'd stuck with either Dr. Bergerac or Dr. Baltimore. It's a low-decibel wistfulness; I can barely hear it over the roar of later, louder regrets. This kind is not so bad, the If I Did One Thing Differently, Then Maybe Everything Would Also Be Different sort, a vague, philosophical itch: yes, if life were different, then life would be different. Such thinking feels like science fiction, stepping on a bug in 20,000 BC and altering the course of history.

Other memories are more troublesome. Here's a length of time, my brain says, and then it stares, it sees an actual *length* of time suspended in the air, which then breaks into panels, as in a comic book. Here I am in one panel. I am in the line of danger, but I don't know it, I am living in the past: the past being defined by the fact that Pudding is alive, but not for long. In the next panel, seconds later, something is supposed to intervene. Superman swooping in, to — what? Deliver the baby? X-ray vision and superhearing are nothing special, every doctor's office comes equipped. Superman is supposed to come is all I know, so Pudding will persist.

But Superman never shows. I can see it so clearly. In one panel we are safe and stupid. In the next we're only stupid.

Those moments come later, toward the end of the pregnancy.

X-rays and interns aside: the real reason I left Dr. Bergerac is that I didn't love him. I wanted to. He was very cute and liked Tintin, and he even spoke English, but he was also authoritative, bossy about my weight, and far preferred talking to Edward (as Dr. Baltimore had far preferred talking to me). Before sonograms, he applied the necessary gel from a squirt bottle as though spraying a graffiti tag, and afterward he dropped wads of paper towels onto me from a height and left me to mop up. He made it clear that if he thought I needed an epidural, I would have one, no matter what. I didn't know what to expect of birth, but I wanted it to seem like a collaboration. So I was delighted when, seven months pregnant, I found an English-speaking midwife through a midwifery Web site, a fox faced woman name Claudelle who shared office space with a yoga instructor in a nearby town. At first I saw her with Dr. Bergerac's blessing: at the Bergerac hospital, my monthly checkups would be with a midwife anyhow, and Claudelle lived much closer to us. At my visits she checked my blood pressure and asked me a variety of questions and once or twice had me bounce on one of the exercise balls she shared with the yoga instructor. I thought I would miss the sonograms, that is, until Claudelle put her hands on my stomach, and described Pudding.

"Ah," she said, rounding the left side of me. "There 'e is. See," she said, and put my hand in place of hers. "There is his back, on the left. A good place. Easy to get down. His head is down here. He's getting ready." Then she got out the stethoscope with the attached speaker and found the old-time radio coconut-shell horse hooves of his heartbeat. "Very good," she said. "You hear? Tout est parfait."

Later that day I felt my stomach. There it was, the hard fact of his back, a sweet, dorsal, infant curve. I had always loved the sentimental science of the ultrasounds, seeing the screen, his bodily essence paradoxically disembodied, his bones decisive, the little snub nose, the lump where Dr. Bergerac had typed *boy,* the heart working away in all of its miraculous clockwork gadgetry. But there was always something Ground-Control-to-Major-Tom about the experience. Deep down, I believed, in the way of moon-landing deniers, that it was all well and good to show me this dim grayscale picture on a screen, but you call that proof? Surely it was a hoax, it had to be a hoax: it was easier to believe it was fake than to accept it was possible, real, done.

Now: my hand, my stomach, his back. A human being. A boy baby. Pudding himself.

The problem was that Claudelle didn't deliver babies anymore: her children had complained about the hours she'd had to keep. Still, she knew a midwife in Bordeaux who did. She called Sylvie and made the appointment for us, since Sylvie didn't speak English. ("The important word is the same," Dr. Bergerac had pointed out. "Poussez, madame.") The next week we drove to Sylvie's office in Bordeaux. Like Claudelle's office, it felt more like the living room of a graduate student in Women's Studies than anything medical.

Sylvie herself was energetic and full of metaphors. Upon checking my cervix, for instance, she announced, The door is closed! The baby is upstairs! When she asked me about pain relief and I said that I'd rather forgo everything, she said, in English, "Strong woman!" and showed her biceps. Best of all, she was willing to come to Savary and pick us up and drive us to the hospital in Bordeaux.

She even said we could have a home birth. I mulled the idea over. To give birth in a farmhouse seemed appealingly Little House on the Prairie. "You are almost forty!" my friend Wendy told me when I asked what she thought. "It's your first pregnancy! You are not allowed to have a home birth!"

She probably had a point.

I told my mother, "So I'm going to have a midwife deliver the baby, but in the hospital."

"Are there doctors in this hospital?" my mother wanted to know.

"Of course."

"Why doesn't one of *them* deliver the baby?" she asked.

But I loved Sylvie's optimism. Why not be optimistic? Everything was going so well. My friend Patti told me I should be the poster girl for Advanced Maternal Age pregnancies. I felt great. I ate intelligently, if a little heavy on the chocolate mousse. My major problems were a touch of sciatica, a touch of pregnancy-induced carpal tunnel syndrome. I got more and more pregnant, blew past my American due date, which was April 18, but the midwives weren't worried: my French due date wasn't until April 27. I paid out of pocket for everything and submitted bills to my American health insurance, and at the end of every appointment, when I was asked for fifteen, or twenty-five, or thirty euros, I wanted to say, "That's adorable!"

Sylvie came to Savary for a last visit. She arrived with a plush stuffed pelvis and a slightly soiled baby doll to act out Pudding's escape route. "Voilà," she said, threading the doll through the pelvis: delivering a baby was like uncorking a bottle of champagne, sometimes you had to twist this way and that before it came free. Then she hooked me up to heart rate and contraction monitors and handed me a game-show-like button on a cable, to press when I felt Pudding move.

"Tout est parfait," said Sylvie. The door was still closed. The baby was still upstairs.

Why worry about due dates? I wasn't even impatient. A neighbor had told us a nightmare story of an alcoholic woman in Ireland she'd known who went two weeks past her due date without telling her doctors, and her child died: starved to death inside of her, really, because her placenta had stopped functioning and no one had noticed. That wouldn't be my problem. In the past week I'd had a fetal monitor strapped to me, and a sonogram, and even an impromptu pelvic X-ray that seemed to be for a good reason.

We were ready for Pudding.

And then the calamity.

Every day of my second pregnancy, I thought of Pudding, of course. But I tried not to think of the exact circumstances of his death. At first I was worried I'd stay in bed weeping, and then I thought: If I remember everything, I'm done for. If I remember, I will walk to the nearest hospital and ask for a nice bed in the psychiatric wing, I promise to be quiet, I promise I will not ask for narcotics, just keep me, nurse, for a few months. In May you can transfer me please to maternity. I am not crazy, but I am being careful: I am not crazy, but if I'm not careful I will take a wrong step and end up in the forest. Sometimes I can feel it happening: my memory, my bad memory, my untrained memory. It creeps toward that time, the end of April 2006, a child warned away from dangers and therefore obsessed by them. Help me. We need to grab it by the scruff of the neck: *not yet*.

Not yet.

It was Maud who told me the story of that tragic drunk woman, and Maud who put me off the close-by hospital in Marmande: her son, Finn, was born there black-and-blue from a hard delivery. Maud, who our landlady paid to look after Savary, was our social life, along with her Anglo-Irish boyfriend, known at the bar where they drank as Jack the Irish Two — there were so many Jack the Irishes that they needed to be numbered. Maud's father, who sometimes visited, was Jack the Irish Three. Jack and Maud lived ten minutes away from us in an old presbytery with Maud's four-year-old daughter, Madeleine, and two-year-old Finn; a lovely lemonade-yellow, lion-headed retriever; and a cat named, by Madeleine, Two-Dogs.

Maud was in her late twenties, with messy boy-cut blond hair and a wicked sense of humor. Jack was about fifty, tall and thin and ponytailed: he looked like the bass player of some band that had been medium big in the 1970s. They both drank a lot. We called them the Sots. They invited us over to dinner parties with their other Anglophone friends: a plumber named Eric and his sad wife, Marie; straw-hatted Ted and his wife, Elaine, who were older and more cheerful; and a voluble, chubby, sexy woman named Lola, who had a Greek boyfriend named Pete. Lola's father was Indian and her mother English; she had caramel skin, striped hair, and an extensive wardrobe of colored contact lenses. The blue ones made her look as though she were developing cataracts, and the green ones as though she were about to turn into the Hulk. Her boyfriend, Pete the Greek, spoke scarcely any English but liked to deliver long monologues about hunting and what he'd learned about American police by watching *Cops:* "America? Gun. Security. Boom: no problem. Person? In house? Gun. Look up. Boom. Fox? No good. So, boom. No dead. Black. Pig. Me, friend, boom boom. No dead." Lola spoke to him in Greek. She was fluent but had such a thick cockney accent that I swore I was always about to understand her — it sounded as though she were saying, "Acropolis Demetrius where to, Guvnor? Sophocles Melanoma, 'ave a pork pie."

The dining room at the presbytery was long and rectangular, filled mostly with a long rectangular table. Everyone smoked. Everyone drank. Even Finn, the two-year-old, a sweet and goofy kid who spoke, as far as I could tell, Esperanto, drank: he had to be stopped from emptying the dregs of beer bottles left on the table. The next carafe of wine was always warming on the woodstove. On winter nights they closed the shutters against the cold, and it was like being sealed up in a wall.

The night of Jack's forty-ninth birthday party fell on the last night of hunting season, and so Pete the Greek wasn't around, having vowed to bag a wild boar. Lola herself had to go home early, to attend to her business: she produced a kind of phone-in television infomercial that showed on English cable. Originally she'd supervised what she said was the first phone-sex call center in England. The problem was, according to her, with all of those women working together in the same room, their periods synchronized, which made for a hellish work environment. Now she dealt in psychics. People watched the show and texted in questions; her hired psychics, in the comfort of their own homes, would have to text back one hundred characters of prophecy. This night she was short a couple of psychics and so had to do an overnight shift herself.

"The number one question," she explained before she left, "is 'Will he come back?' But you get everything. When is the next Al Qaeda attack, will I meet the love of my life next week, another psychic says he will come back, can you confirm, do you have a message from my dead grandpa."

"What do you say?" I asked.

Her eyes were khaki green that night. "Well, sometimes you sort of get an image, and you tell them, 'I see an old coat and a rainbow and an empty bottle.' It's amazing how often that's really meaningful to someone."

I couldn't tell whether *amazing* meant she was amazed at her psychic abilities or the nature of coincidence or the ability of a desperate mind to find meaning in a random assortment of visuals. I thought about asking her if I could help out one night, though I never worked up the nerve. I liked the idea of trying to summarize someone's best dreams in a handful of characters, a kind of augural haiku. That's how I saw my role in fortune-telling. I had no need of psychics myself. I knew my future.

Then Maud was pregnant, too. "Christmas!" she said, as though Christmas were a famous time for getting accidentally pregnant.

She made for a very strange pregnancy support group. Though she was a smart woman and the daughter of a doctor, any good sense she had was clouded by the fact that she drank and spent all of her time with people who drank. How could she stop? The winter was too cold not to drink, the spring too lovely, the summer too bakingly hot. She told me in all seriousness that the more pregnant you were, the more you could drink, and that after three months there was no danger, because the baby was already "fully formed." The doctor father, who we never met, was apparently also a great drinker, and perhaps his prenatal advice was likewise shaped by his feeling that it would be a shame to deny his daughter anything that might quench her considerable thirst. Her pregnancy intake was modest compared to what she'd been drinking before. That is, whenever I saw her she drank four or five beers. She smoked, too. At dinner parties Jack was very shy and sat at the end of the table rolling perfect cigarettes two at a time, one for him and one for her.

It was upsetting to watch. And yet I liked Maud anyhow, which shows you that I could rationalize as much as she did. She was otherwise kind and funny, and I wondered if she'd imagined that this would be her life, in exile in France with two children and another coming, dead broke all the time, in love with the second drunk in a row, a man who himself had two daughters back in England. Maud could not give up drinking, and so convinced herself it was not so bad; I could not give up my fondness for Maud, and so I tried to think of her drinking as a mildly entertaining eccentricity. She thought I was crazy for not drinking, or maybe she just thought I was American and therefore a bit of a priss. And I'm afraid I compared my own prenatal habits to Maud's and felt superior. Surely I was doing everything right, everything you needed to do to have a healthy baby.

We saw them last a few days after Pudding died: we met at their bar, the Café du Commerce, in the next town over, the town whose name I cannot remember and refuse to look up. I dreaded it. For a few months Maud's daughter's greatest pleasure was to say to me, "You have a GREAT BIG BELLY." I thought it was possible that if Madeleine said anything to me about my stomach, I'd punch her in the face, and I did not want to be a woman who punched four-year-olds in the face. We sat outside under the arcades.

All winter long my American friends who heard my stories about the Sots found it hilarious that Jack and Maud knew only the teetotaling me: I like a drink myself, under ordinary circumstances. These were not ordinary circumstances, either. I gulped beer and smoked, and Finn and Madeleine as usual ran around and rifled through the postcard stands of the *tabac* next door, and Madeleine didn't say anything, and I remembered two weeks before, when we'd been at the presbytery and Finn stripped himself naked and climbed up onto my chair and stood next to me, and I put my hand on his bare little bottom, and thought, *This is what having a little boy will be like,* and thought, *Oh, I'm ready.*

Maud had a little girl last September, named Mia. That's all I know.

T he first thing we did back at Savary was dismantle the future. That is, Edward broke down the portable crib that had been waiting for a few weeks on my side of the bed. I threw out all my maternity clothes, just threw them away, along with the single package of diapers I'd obediently bought (my baby book warned me that you could never be really sure how big your newborn would be). We tossed out the stuffed hippopotamus from Edward's sister and any other toylike object. For a month I'd fallen asleep looking at an old artist's palette that had been painted to look like a grinning face, like Punch in profile. Another flea market find, we'd hung it over the crib. That we burned in a bonfire out back, along with the baby books.

But not the baby clothes.

The baby clothes had crowded out mine in my chest of drawers. There were the silly things I'd bought him, ludicrous, adorable, irreplaceable. A pair of plaid plus fours. A striped turtleneck with a picture of Babar. A thick blue and brown coat with toggle closures. Those leather baby shoes. An Iowa Hawkeyes onesie, his first present, which our friends Tim and Wendy had brought when they came to visit. A Union Jack hat from Catherine, my sister-in-law, along with a 1940s-style cloth coat. Two beautiful tiny sweaters knit by Edward's mother. Bibs. Socks. About half the clothes were hand-me-downs from a little boy named Owen who lived in Cambridge, Massachusetts, who was outgrowing things faster than his mother could keep up.

Who can separate practicality from hope from lingering superstition? We wanted another child. We wanted to fill those clothes.

And so, without even looking, we packed them away, three boxes full. We could throw them out later, if we had to.

That afternoon we called the movers, who were going to take our boxes to Edward's parents' house in England. They were supposed to come in five days, but we hadn't settled on an actual time. The owner of the business, an English guy in his thirties, had been over to the house two weeks before to give us an estimate. A lifetime ago. We'd talked about babies. His son had been born in Bordeaux, too, with kidney problems. The hospital was good, he'd said. Now Edward left a message with the receptionist at the moving company explaining what had happened.

"It doesn't need to be mentioned again," said Edward. "I just wanted him to know ahead of time so he won't ask."

The owner called back later that day, all business, to say that he'd be over the next morning to take our stuff.

"I thought Monday," said Edward.

No, said the mover, this was it, their one trip for the month.

"You do understand what we've gone through," said Edward cautiously.

Yes, he did.

It was Thursday. I checked the voicemail, sure that he'd said Monday. He had.

Edward called back.

Well, said the mover, then that was a mistake, but that's how it is.

It seemed too much to bear. How could we be expected to buy packing tape when our child had died? To pack in eighteen hours what we'd thought we'd had three days to do? To stay up all night sealing up cartons, for someone else's mistake? I was furious, insane at the injustice of having to deal with anything even mildly difficult in the face of the hardest thing in the world. "When," I asked Edward, as we drove to buy more tape, "did we become characters in a Raymond Carver story?"

We spent the day packing and cursing the mover. It was invigorating to have such a villain. I didn't care about his carelessness, only his cowardice: if he'd abjectly apologized I would have forgiven him. "I'm going to tell him," I told Edward.

"Good."

"I'm going to say, I just hope no one is ever this cruel to your wife, or your child."

"I think you should."

"I'll say, How would *you* feel — "

But he sent over a single hired hand to do the work, and I was spared the pleasure.

At night when I'm tired I still write him angry letters in my head before I fall asleep.

We didn't want to go back to Bordeaux after Pudding died, but we had to: the autopsy took three days, and only then could we pick up Pudding's body, to accompany it to the crematorium. On the way to the morgue we had to stop at a pharmacy so poor Edward could negotiate a tube of hemorrhoid cream for me. (Sometimes, when I think back on those days I forget that I wasn't just a woman who had lost a child, I had given birth to one, too, and was recovering.) This was the last of Bordeaux. We hated the place. It was ruined for us worse than the rest of France was. Edward had mentioned to his parents that we'd like to spend the summer in North Norfolk, near the sea, and within forty-eight hours they had found a cottage for rent in a small town called Holt. It wasn't free for three weeks, but it felt like a miracle: we had somewhere to go.

The morgue was just by the hospital. It felt — well, dead, but dead in an early-morning dentist's-office way, clean and deserted. The waiting room was large and sparsely furnished, with a coffee vending machine by the plate glass windows at the front and a windowless double door into the back. We rang a bell; a woman came to see what we wanted; we gave the name in its mangled aitchless French version: R-Vay.

You may see the child again, she said.

We'd been warned by the funeral director that we'd be asked this. No thank you, we told her.

Well then, she said. Please wait.

We sat. It was very sunny out, but the room was so big that the light from all those windows at the front stalled out at the coffee machine. It was in no danger of getting anywhere near us. I remember craning my head to look at the outside. At first there was nothing, and then the most funereal person I have ever seen in my life walked by, a Gallic Boris Karloff. He wore a white dress shirt. His shoulders had a sorrowful hunch. His dark overhanging eyebrows looked carved from granite, like tombstones, monuments to worry. Of course he had something to do with the morgue: he couldn't have gone into anything but a funerary profession. Maybe this was the family face, and the family business, and who could say whether it was evolution or destiny or an acceptance that one's face is one's fortune, or misfortune.

"That's the screws," said Edward.

"What?"

"That's the sound of them screwing the lid down," and then I could hear the dim sound of a turning power tool. That was good. It meant we didn't have to wait much longer.

Of course Boris Karloff turned out to be the hearse driver. I couldn't understand a single word of his French, he mumbled so apologetically. The hearse was a plainish station wagon. He gave directions to the cemetery. Edward seemed to understand him.

We followed the car, a threadbare funeral procession. At every rotary the cemetery was marked, but we checked the map anyhow. What could be worse than to lose sight of our boy now?

In the middle of the cemetery, Boris Karloff pulled up in front of a building that housed both the crematorium and a few chapels for funerals. He shook our hands and directed us inside. The building had the timeless feel of an institutional edifice constructed in good taste, with no heart. It might have been erected in 1952 or 1977 or 2005. The funeral director greeted us. We said our name, we said we were the R-Vays, and he indicated with his hand the direction to walk.

At every turn of the hallway was a sign with the international line drawing of a martini glass, the kind that indicates airport cocktail lounges, underscored with an arrow, though if you followed them you got only as far as a vending machine for bottled water. There was another funeral going on that day, for a grown-up, and we walked against the current of mourners who seemed to be taking it all very well.

The director brought us into our chapel.

I am sorry, he said, for the size of the room, but it is all we have.

The size of the room was vast, appropriate for the service of someone very famous, or very friendly, or very old, someone who could attract mourner after mourner. Surely they should have put the other funeral here, I thought, but maybe they weighed the possibilities and decided: to put fifty people in a room meant for two hundred is sadder than putting two people there.

This way, said the funeral director, and he brought us to the front, where the casket had been set on a cabinet. We had seen the casket only in a catalog at the funeral home by the hospital. The director said, I will leave you for a moment.

"It's too big," I said when he'd gone.

"I know," said Edward, looking at the room yawning out behind us. It upset him. "If I were my father, I'd complain—"

But I'd meant the casket. A brass plate had been fixed to the top: *Pudding Harvey, 2006*. I wondered how caskets came. I mean how they were sized. We'd chosen the cheapest casket, the cheapest urn. Now we touched the wood very tentatively. What age was this meant for? For a child, surely, not a baby, and it made me sad that he, who had so little to his name, was lying inside such a big, empty, dark space. I didn't like to think of where he was in there, at the top, at the bottom, but I wondered. It should have fit him.

It would be burned too, of course, with the brass plate.

Again we had to nod at a French stranger and say, Yes, that's fine, you may carry him away now. The cremation itself would take some time. We sat outside at a distance from the building and smoked cigarettes. After a while we realized we were sitting in the patch of land reserved for the scattering of remains, and we moved. At another time in our lives we might have been horrified. Now we just slapped the dust off the seat of our pants and moved on.

Who would scatter ashes here? The lazy? The unambitious? You stumble from the crematorium, and say, Well, here's as good a place as any? We were having Pudding cremated because we wanted to take him out of France, and it was easier to do so in an urn than in a coffin, and we didn't know where we'd bury him. My father had suggested the graveyard outside the church at the bottom of Edward's parents' driveway, where we'd been married, but when I thought about it I didn't want to feel sad every time we drove past. We'd scatter them somewhere beautiful, once we'd come up with the right place. Surely that was the point of cremation: you could take your beloved anywhere, let him rest anywhere, not just walk out the door and chuck. I didn't understand.

Maybe you just couldn't afford a burial: the embalming, the plot, the stone.

Maybe you just wanted to be done with the whole sad business, you'd attended to your dying relative for months or years, or you'd had a long life with him, too long, in fact. You wanted to fling your sorrow over your shoulder and never look back.

We didn't want to get it over with; it would take months for us to scatter his ashes. For now we found some clean grass and sat and smoked and flicked those lighter ashes into the air. After half an hour, we walked back in. The funeral director demonstrated our new possessions: the ashes, which were inside an urn with another plaque underneath that said *Pudding Harvey, Bordeaux, 2006,* which slipped into an innocuous blue nylon bag, and a certificate explaining to suspicious customs agents what the substance was. We thanked him.

"I want to pry that plaque off with a knife," said Edward as we left. "I don't want the word *Bordeaux* anywhere near him."

We got in a car and headed for the *rocade,* the highway that girdled the city, for the last time in our lives.

When I was a teenager in Boston, a man on the subway handed me a card printed with tiny pictures of hands spelling out the alphabet in sign language. I AM DEAF, said the card. You were supposed to give the man some money in exchange.

I have thought of that card ever since, during difficult times, mine or someone else's: surely when tragedy has struck you dumb, you should be given a stack of cards that explain it for you. When Pudding died, I wanted my stack. I still want it. *My first child was stillborn,* it would say on the front. It remains the hardest thing for me to explain, even now, or maybe I mean especially now — now that his death feels like a non sequitur. *My first child was stillborn.* I want people to know but I don't want to say it aloud. People don't like to hear it but I think they might not mind reading it on a card.

I could have taken my cards, translated into French, to the stores of Duras, where the baker, the butcher, the dry cleaner, the grocery store ladies, had seen me growing bigger and bigger over the months: I couldn't bear the idea of them seeing me deflated and asking after the baby. "Voilà," I'd say, and hand over a card. I could have given a card to the imperious man at immigration in Portsmouth who almost denied me entry into England. To the waiter at the curry house that summer who was always mean to us. To the receptionist at the ob-gyn practice in Saratoga Springs at my first visit. To the nurses who asked me why I was scheduled for such close prenatal monitoring.

To every single person who noticed I was pregnant the second time, and said, "Congratulations! Is this your first?"

To every person who peeks into the stroller now and says the same thing.

Every day of my life, I think, I'll meet someone and be struck dumb, and all I'll have to do is reach in my pocket.

This book, I am just thinking now, is that card.

When I called my friend Ann the first time after Pudding died, she immediately asked what she could do, and then did everything, and then kept asking, and she sent out an e-mail to tell people I hadn't told that was so beautiful — though I have never read it — that I got the most beautiful condolence notes in response. Wendy burst into hysterical tears at the sound of my voice and asked me questions until I'd told the whole story. "Was he a beautiful baby?" she wanted to know, and I wondered how she knew to ask: she was the only one who did. Margi said, "Oh, Elizabeth, please know that if any of us could absorb your pain for you, we would," and then laughed at all my dark jokes. Bruce, remembering something just as terrible that had happened to him decades before, wrote, "There is no way for such an event to leave you who you are." Patti, who has seen as much sorrow as anyone I know, was an extraordinary combination of complete sympathy and complete comprehension. My brother said, at the end of a long conversation, "Well, I guess as a family we've been pretty lucky that we haven't had something awful happen before." My sister-in-law Catherine texted, *Poor poor darling you*.

Somehow every one of these things happened at exactly the right time for me. This is why you need everyone you know after a disaster, because there is not one right response. It's what paralyzes people around the grief-stricken, of course, the idea that there are right things to say and wrong things and it's better to say nothing than something clumsy.

I needed all of it, direct comfort, hearsay grief. Edward's great friend Claudia's husband, Arno, a stage manager and perhaps the calmest man I've ever met, burst into tears on the phone when Edward called, and when Ann called my friends Jonathan and Lib, Jonathan did, too. "Oh," Ann said to me, "to hear that big man cry." I couldn't have borne listening myself, to him or Arno, but to know that they did — it felt as though they had taken part of the weeping weight from my shoulders. Of course I cried an awful lot, but I also regretted every stupid time I'd ever cried in my life before over *nothing,* days as a teenager I'd wept myself sick and couldn't exactly remember why, when I should have saved up. Now, in Tipperary and near Harvard Square, big men were crying for us. Before this I'd imagined that professional mourners, people hired to cry at funerals, were always little old ethnic grandmothers, maybe because the first funeral I'd been to was for a fifth-grade classmate named Paula Leone, and her Italian aunts had howled at the graveside.

"They shouldn't be old women," I told Edward in Bordeaux. "They should be big men, a whole line of them, crying."

I *don't know what to say,* people wrote, or, *Words fail.*

What amazed me about all the notes I got — mostly through e-mail, because who knew how to find me? — was how people *did* know what to say, how words *didn't* fail. Even the words *words fail* comforted me. Before Pudding died, I'd thought condolence notes were simply small bits of old-fashioned etiquette, important but universally acknowledged as inadequate gestures. Now they felt like oxygen, and only now do I fully understand why: to know that other people were sad made Pudding more real. My friend Rob e-mailed me first, a beautiful and straightforward vow to do anything he could to help me. Some people apologized for sending sympathy through the ether; some overnighted notes; it made no difference to me. I read them, and reread them. They made me cry, which helped. They *moved* me, that is to say, they felt physical, they budged me from the sodden self-disintegrating lump I otherwise was. As I was going mad from grief, the worst of it was that sometimes I believed I was making it all up. Here was some proof that I wasn't.

One day Ann wrote to say that people, even people who didn't know me, had asked what they could do for me.

"They could write," I told her. I considered this a sign of my essential mental health, that I could both think of something that would make me feel better and ask for it.

The English Department head at Skidmore, Linda Simon, was one of the people who'd asked, and soon enough my e-mail box filled up with messages from my future colleagues. I'd met some but not others, and every single message meant the world. One, from a famous writer who taught in the department, was so eloquent that it inspired in me the only moment of true denial I remember from that terrible time: I thought, *I'll save this, and show it to Pudding when he's older: it'll really mean something to him.*

People speak of losing friends when someone dear to them dies, but we were lucky. I lost only one friend, and possibly she doesn't even know it yet, and probably I'd lost her long before. Her mother had died when this friend was a teenager, her father died when she was in her thirties. Frankly, I'd been good to her after her father's death, though by the time Pudding died we were no longer as close as we'd been. One of my best friends called to tell her my bad news and then e-mailed to say that he had done so.

I waited to hear from her. And waited.

It took three months. That would have been all right if

she'd said, *I didn't know what to say,* or *I'm sorry, I've been trying to find the words.*

"I was hoping to speak to you," she wrote, "or be able to send a paper letter, but I don't have a number or address for you, and I simply couldn't wait any longer."

It's hard to explain the rage I felt at reading this, at her attempt to turn her silence into something noble, when all of my other friends had turned themselves inside out to help me months before. The entire note was full of platitudes. "Losing a child is the worst pain one can experience, I think," she wrote, and I hated her for that *I think,* as though she wanted to make it seem as though my pain was her original thought, a theory she'd honed in social work school. Even now I realize how petty I'm being, how the only problem was that she'd waited too long to write the note. Her shock and sympathy were no longer fresh, and her language reflected that. But my grief was still fresh, grief lasts longer than sympathy, which is one of the tragedies of the grieving, and the distance between what I felt and what she wrote infuriated me.

She's written to me since. I have never written back.

O h, Elizabeth," my friend Lib wrote, "these past ten months did happen, Pudding did happen, we won't forget him. He's part of our family, one of those cousins or great-aunts that not everyone has met but is still part of the whole damn sweet sad picture."

My friend Lib is a baby freak. I hadn't realized that before, though we've known each other for twenty years now, ever since we were little library workers together at the Newton Free Library in Newton, Massachusetts. All through my pregnancy with Pudding, she hovered over me through the phone wires, asking questions and giving sound advice on matters ranging from education to what sort of underpants one might need postpartum. Edward and I stay with Lib and Jonathan and their daughters, Sophie and Nora, when we're in Boston: it's a sweet house full of snacks and nice girls and good books, and we'd been looking forward to introducing Pudding to it.

Lib e-mailed me all the time, after Pudding died. We

spoke for hours on the phone, too, but the phone conversations have gone wherever conversations go, up in a mist of white wine, and the French sun, and the smoke off a ferry headed to England, and the English seaside. She was not normally a writer of e-mails — her daughters were eleven and five, and the computer was on the third floor of their house — but she wrote to me then. She still writes to me about Pudding. She misses him like a person too, I think.

I want to explain to her daughters what their mother did for me. I think in some ways she saved my life.

But I can't explain, I can only give examples.

She wrote, "We spent the evening with Adam, all crying softly into his birthday bourbon, it may not be strictly Kubler-Ross but hell we really don't have a vocabulary for this kind of loss. I think I'll take Nora's lead on this one. When she learned that Pudding died she clamped her hands over her ears, stamped her feet and yelled no more people dying. Now, she carries him around and sleeps with him, his name is Owen Alexander Green and she says Elizabeth and Edward don't have to worry because she is taking care of him. Nora's world is a beautiful place."

She wrote, "I woke up today thinking of you. It's Mother's Day, Elizabeth. Of course I'm thinking of how I desperately wish circumstances were different. But I'm also thinking about how connected we all are, all us mothers. The old ones, the new ones, the sad, the crazy, Natalie, Cornelia and we Elizabeths. I'm thinking I feel very close to you, to

Pudding, to your grief and to mine. I looked forward to seeing his face, the combining of you two dear people. The image I hold of him now is of a chubby baby at the water in his mother's arms, she's trying to get him to touch the water but he pulls up his little fat legs, retracts them in an 'I'd rather not' sort of a way. Deborah, my midwife friend, says that of the women she's known whose babies have died, of course all of them wish life had unfolded differently, but none wished that they hadn't carried, loved, and birthed those children. Those are some amazing mothers. You are one amazing mother. I love you very much this day."

She wrote, "It's hard to be with grief. We all so want to help and there is really nothing to do. My crazy adored aunt Pauline's catchphrase was 'offer it up.' Those words were a curse, a joke, a prayer and a balm to us cousins over the years. Whack your funny bone, lose your engagement ring, catch your boyfriend cheating, lower your mother's body into the ground and offer it up. I catch myself these days offering it up, driving around saying out loud 'Pudding, what the fuck?' An infant in the ice cream shop almost brought me to my knees yesterday. I breathed her in and tenderly offered it up."

She wrote, "At security in Copenhagen on the return trip an extended Middle Eastern family were bidding tearful good-byes to the ancient mother and father. The old lady from ethnic-old-lady central casting, bless her heart, kissed everyone soundly on the cheeks. The babes she held tight, kissed on the cheeks, and planted a big wet one right on their hearts. Well, that did it for me, started bawling quietly and discreetly on the chaotic airport spot. How's your heart old friend. I'm thinking of you a lot and sending many heart kisses."

It's the last days in Savary where my memory starts to get oceanic: it shifts, it suddenly dips, it drops out of view and then comes over my head in a wave. I splutter, my mouth full of the stuff. We drank a lot of wine on the patio. We cried a lot. We watched every meaningless video in our collection. I checked my e-mail all the time. I needed to know who was worried about me. I've reread some of the e-mails I wrote back to friends recently, and I'm astounded by how chipper I sound; I even find them slightly creepy, and I wonder if my friends did, too. I remember one long phone conversation with my brother during which I walked around and around the L-shaped dining room table in the L-shaped dining room (diners at one end wouldn't be able to see diners at the other end) touching the back of each chair; I hung up the phone loving my brother even more than I had before, but now I can't recall a word that either of us said. My parents arrived a few days later — they'd scheduled the trip months before to meet Pudding — and I remember almost nothing of that visit other than one day we had a great deal to drink at lunch, and then we all took very long naps, and then Edward made Ovaltine and toast for dinner.

The day my parents left, we left Savary for good and began traveling.

But before this, we had one day — this is very strange, it's the last day I remember really clearly — when somehow everything was slightly better. Not all right at all, but one day we made jokes and actually laughed at them. A day of grace. We knew that something very, very terrible had happened, but it seemed to have happened to someone else, perhaps to someone very dear to people dear to us, a friend of a friend we'd always heard stories about. There was sadness in the house, but it didn't have us by the throat. Even as it happened, I wondered what it meant. Was it possible that already we were returning to ourselves?

Things got much worse after that.

The journey from Duras to Holt — from the farmhouse by a vineyard in France to a four-bedroom cottage not too far from the North Sea — was Odyssean. That felt right. It felt good to do hard physical travel away from . . . away from everything. First we drove north to a small village near Angoulême, where we spent two nights with old friends of Edward's — dear friends of mine now, too — and where I was very poor company.

Then we drove to Nantes, to drop off our rented Peugeot. Then we caught a train, and then a bus, to Roscoff, where we spent the night in a hotel looking over the harbor and wandered around all day until it was time to catch the overnight ferry to England. We got off at Portsmouth and took the train to Penzance, where Edward's parents picked us up. We spent three nights at their time-share in Cornwall, where I continued to be poor company, rode with them to London, two nights there, took the train to Suffolk, where we met up with Edward's parents again at their house. Three days later, in my mother-in-law's loaned VW, we drove to Holt.

Somewhere in there was Mother's Day. We were with the friends near Angoulême. I lurked in a far doorway and smoked and drank wine by myself. My parents were still in France, and I had to call my mother to wish her a happy day, but I didn't want to. Was I a mother, I asked myself, and despite Lib's beautiful e-mail I still don't know the answer. I want to tell that sad version of myself, *Of course you're a mother, just one who's learned a hard lesson*. I want to tell that sad version of myself, *I'm sorry, no, it's tough luck, he died before you met him, people keep track of such things, and if we call you a mother, then where does it stop?* It was the uncertainty that seemed unbearable to me. Even now. This year I had a very glorious baby with me, but was it my first Mother's Day, or my second?

Those weeks were miserable with company and travel, with luggage and making conversation, but they were forward movement. One step farther, one step farther.

We almost had to take one mammoth step back. Immigration at the ferry terminal in Portsmouth was a single thin man behind a single thin podium. His days must have been dull, waving on one EU passport after another, the French coming to England, the English returning home, an occasional intrepid German, none of whom could be stopped and questioned. When he saw my U.S. passport, he perked up.

"Are you traveling alone?"

"No," I said. I gestured to Edward, who'd gone ahead. "With my husband, who's an English citizen."

This is, by the way, not a useful thing to say, and it's not the first time I've gotten in trouble with Her Majesty's Border Guards: three and a half years before, a woman at Heathrow asked me the purpose of my visit, and I had said, cheerily, "I'm getting married!" The English are as suspicious of undocumented spouses of citizens as the Americans are: they worry you will assume a certain level of privilege and never get around to sorting yourself out legally. At Heathrow the woman made me sit down on a bench for a long time, next to an athlete from Ghana who was likewise waiting for clearance, and let me through only after a long lecture about not overstaying my six-month tourist allowance. In Portsmouth, the thin border guard perked up further, in the manner of a dog who, already sitting up straight, sits up straighter to show that he's obeying a command and deserves a biscuit. In fact he looked like a Jack Russell terrier with dreams of being promoted to bloodhound. He began to leaf through my passport.

"It looks to me as though you've spent most of the last two years in the United Kingdom," he said with a certain joy. I couldn't figure out how he'd arrived at this theory.

"No," I answered truthfully. "Three weeks a year, at the most."

"Well, that's not what it looks like to me," he said.

We went back and forth. My years as a librarian always help me in such situations: I am very good at keeping my cool with officious, insistent strangers, though my training is on the other side of the desk. I was miraculously polite. Even so it seemed for a while that he might put me on the next ferry back to France. *What will I do?* I wondered. I pictured myself alone on the ferry, having been manhandled on board by some as yet unseen immigration thug. I tried to explain myself, I tried to remember the exact dates and circumstances of my handful of visits to England. Again and again he told me that it seemed that I'd been illegally living in the United Kingdom. I shifted from foot to foot for forty-five minutes as he did his best to catch me in an inconsistency.

When, exactly, might we be moved to unpack the shoulder bag, show him the death certificate of very recent vintage, open the tiny blue nylon sack, and pull out the wooden urn of ashes with the brass plaque underneath that said, *Pudding Harvey, Bordeaux, 2006?* Look, we might have said, something terrible has happened to us. Grant us a tiny bit of grace no matter what you think.

Two things saved us. First, I explained that Edward

planned to immigrate to the United States at the end of the summer.

"Have you begun that process?" he said.

I reeled off the name and number of every single form I'd filled out.

Then he asked us what we did for a living, and I said tiredly, "We're writers."

He perked up again, like a Jack Russell terrier who dreams of being a famous Jack Russell terrier. I'd seen that look before: *As it happens, I fancy myself a writer.*

"Books?" he asked.

"Yes," I said. "I've published three, and my husband has published two."

That seemed to do the trick. He took down the particulars of my passport, stamped it, wrote down a code, and waved us through. We were almost free when he called out—

"Would I find your books in a bookstore?"

"Yes," I said as pleasantly as I could, backing away from him. I could smile for only so long. I was worried I'd wasted my year's supply on this man.

Here is a character from a gothic novel: the woman with the stillborn child. Her hair is matted and black. Ghosts nest in it. Her white nightgown is mottled with blood. In her hands is an awful bundle: the corpse she cannot bear to put down. She sings lullabies to it, rocks it in her arms. She says in a pleasant but tremulous voice, *Would you like to see my baby? He's such a nice little baby. Such a little, little baby. Shh: he's sleeping.*

Maybe she's a ghost, dead in childbirth herself. Better hope for that. Ghosts are terrifying but not so bad as a woman ruined by the death of her child.

I was not that woman in the months after Pudding's death. I didn't weep in company. I mostly didn't mention the fact that I had been pregnant, that everything in my life was supposed to be different. I felt bad that I made people feel bad for me. I was corseted by politeness: I could feel my organs, rearranged by pregnancy, squeezed now in completely different directions.

But I felt like that gothic character. At least, I felt like people looked at me as though I were, whenever I did mention the baby or his death or my pregnancy. I could almost see myself with my uncombed hair and filthy nightgown, the tiny corpse in a winding sheet in my arms, walking down a nineteenth-century street as I knocked on doors. I could hear my voice: *Would you like to see my baby?*

This for the merest reference to what had happened to me.

I was a character from an opera who might at any moment let loose with an aria, and generally people tried to cover it up with conversational ragtime. People changed the subject. They smiled uncomfortably. Some tried extraordinary juggling acts, with flung torches of chitchat and spinning scimitars of small talk.

They didn't mention it. They did not say, *I am so sorry* or *How are you?*

I felt in those first weeks, meeting people I knew, like the most terrifying object on earth.

Who knows what other people think? Not me, and especially not then. Still it surprised me, every time I saw someone who didn't mention it. I am writing this and trying to remember how it felt at the time, and trying to imagine what people were thinking. I am trying to remember what I have thought when I've done the same thing, all those times *I* didn't mention some great sadness upon seeing someone for the first time. Did I really think that by not saying words of consolation aloud, I was doing people a favor? As though to mention sadness I was "reminding" them of the terrible thing?

As though the grieving have forgotten their grief?

I remember one lunch with people who loved us in London early on, two of the most excruciating hours of my life. Nothing but that endless juggling: Other people's jobs and boyfriends. What kind of wine to order. This was two weeks after Pudding died. I might have been something like that gothic character one step short of total ruin: I wanted to rock and sing lullabies and hold out my torn, bloody nightgown and run my hands through my wild hair, and yet I knew you weren't supposed to do such things in polite society. My hair *was* uncombed, and my face was puffy from lack of sleep and crying and too much wine, and my clothes were what I'd salvaged from the middle of my pregnancy, because of course even though people might pretend nothing was out of the ordinary I had the body of a woman two weeks postpartum, soft and wide around the middle, and if I'd been one step worse off I might have lifted my shirt up to display my still livid stretch marks.

But I didn't. I could feel how uncomfortable my mere presence made people feel, and I couldn't bear it. So I sat in this Indian restaurant and listened. Sometimes a piece of palaver came loose and shot straight toward me, and somehow I caught it and tossed it back.

All the while, all I could think was: *Dead baby dead baby dead baby.*

And I know everyone around that table was thinking the same thing, every single person.

I've never gotten over my discomfort at other people's discomfort. When people say, What have you been up to, I hesitate. I will tell myself, *Now, if this were a husband or father or sister who died, you wouldn't simply omit the fact.* If I say anything, people mostly change the subject anyway, and I can't say that I blame them.

I've done it myself, when meeting the grief-struck. It's as though the sad news is Rumpelstiltskin in reverse. To mention it by name is to conjure it up, not the grief but the experience itself: the mother's suicide, the brother's overdose, the multiple miscarriages. The sadder the news, the less likely people are to mention it. The moment I lost my innocence about such things, I saw how careless I'd been myself.

I don't even know what I would have wanted someone to say. Not: It will be better. Not: You don't think you'll live through this, but you will. Maybe: Tomorrow you will spontaneously combust. Tomorrow, finally, your misery will turn to wax and heat and you will burn and melt till nothing is left in your chair but a greasy, childless smudge. That might have comforted me.

We'd chosen North Norfolk because Edward had grown up there. We'd rented the smallest four-bedroom house in the world: three of the bedrooms held only a single bed and a table. Edward shimmied a desk into one of the rooms; I wrote sitting up in bed in another. One of the ways in which we felt

— not lucky, not *that* word again —

Let me say we were glad we were free agents and could go somewhere neutral for several months, neither the place we'd lived while waiting for our child, nor the place we would spend the rest of our lives without him.

In that small Norfolk town, we spent one week drinking heavily and smoking, and then we gave ourselves a shake, switched to a fish diet, daily exercise, and work. We had time to kill; until the U.S. government sorted out Edward's immigration application, he was not strictly speaking supposed to travel to the States. We were writers: we wrote. Edward worked on his enormous Parisian novel; I went back to a novel beginning I'd been fiddling around with before I was pregnant, which (I'd forgotten) featured a dead infant. Strangely enough, I was glad for that fictional baby who I'd in all innocence murdered (drowned in a bathtub) a year before: I couldn't have made him up in my grief, but I could pour my grief into him. I wrote a hundred pages of the book and two new short stories; I worked harder and faster than I had in years. At night we watched movies, straight out of the care packages Ann sent me: all of Carole Lombard, all of Mae West, enough silly distraction to last the summer.

Some days were worse than others. For about a week I got the opening line of an Auden poem that I'd memorized in high school stuck in my head: *About suffering they were never wrong, the Old Masters . . .* The poem describes the Breughel painting *The Fall of Icarus,* in which (as Auden explains) life goes on despite the tiny white legs kicking up in the corner of a harbor, Icarus sunk. My high school English teacher had explained that the myth was about hubris, ignoring the good advice of your wise father, but for me that summer the painting, the poem, everything, was about lost boys and the parents who'd failed them. One of the BBC channels was showing Steven Spielberg movies, mother after mother failing to protect her son: *AI* is bad, *Empire of the Sun* is worse, and *E.T.* the worst of all: I sobbed on the sofa at the end of it.

We ate local crab and local seaweed. We swam at Holkham Beach, an amazing stretch of sand that Edward remembered from his boyhood. We went to pubs. We saw children everywhere, of course, and babies. And Edward would always say, "I hope we can have another child," and I would answer, "Me, too."

Work, walks, wine. Our life as usual, having moved to a new place. We got to know our fishmonger and butcher and greengrocer, picked out our restaurants, opened a bottle of wine at 6:00 p.m. if we were cooking at home. On the one hand it was comforting and even lovely, especially the long walks we took along the Norfolk coast, and on the other hand the very usualness, the loveliness, the freedom to do what we wanted, was a kind of torture: look at your unencumbered selves. After most deaths, I imagine, the awfulness lies in how everything's changed: you no longer recognize the form of your days. There's a hole. It's person-shaped and it follows you everywhere, to bed, to the dinner table, in the car.

For us what was killing was how nothing had changed. We'd been waiting to be transformed, and now here we were, back in our old life.

Years before I'd given away an antique postcard that said, beneath a drawing of a pine branch:

For thee I pine.
For thee I balsam.

(I regretted giving away that postcard almost immediately. The recipient didn't deserve it. Me in a nutshell: I don't regret a single instance of giving away my heart, but a novelty postcard with a really good pun? I *still* wish I hadn't.)

Now I pined, and pined. I pictured myself: a pine tree. The trail of the lonesome pine. I saw myself green and leaning on the beach, inclined toward my unreachable darling. To be deciduous would be better. I could stand brown and brittle, and then naked, and then in the spring I would start over again.

Actually, that's sort of what happened.

At the end of August we packed up the few things we'd brought with us to Holt. For the first time in our lives, we had not accumulated a single thing in a new country. We spent a few days in Suffolk, with Edward's family, then a few days in London, then a few days in Boston. On September 5 we paid movers to clear out my vast storage space in Boston, all the things I hadn't seen in four years, and we drove to Saratoga Springs. The rented house we'd arranged by e-mail months before (when Pudding was still alive) was in a bad state, with cigarette butts and condom wrappers and a fly-infested garbage can. The previous tenants had been smokers, and someone had tried to cover the smell with a quantity of Febreze, and then, when that failed, several spilled boxes of mothballs. Up until then we'd had good luck renting places sight unseen, so odds were it was time for us to land hard, but it felt like ominous luck. Moreover, the house belonged to a retired professor from the English Department who lived out of state, and I saw how quickly I could become a villain if I broke the lease. The movers arrived and unloaded our stuff into the house; we couldn't figure out what else to do. When they finally left, I went upstairs to the bathroom and took the pregnancy test I'd been carrying around in my purse all day, and brought it down to the kitchen as it developed to show Edward.

Well, what do you know. This baby would be due in May.

But before this:

The day we left Holt we got up at 5:00 a.m. and drove to Holkham, the wide, bowl-shaped beach of Edward's childhood and of our summer. On the way there, hares jumped along the side of the roads — early risers? going home to their burrows after a night of hell-raising? — and I prayed I wouldn't hit one, that this wouldn't be the first day I struck something living with a car. I didn't believe in omens anymore, but still. We worried that someone else would have beat us to the beach. In England there's always some preposterous superannuated sweetheart with a dog tramping along. But we walked through the scrub pines to the sand and then over the great expanse of sand to the water's edge all alone.

The sky was peach and gold, a teacup of a morning, just enough clouds so as not to mock us. Why isn't there a dawnish equivalent for the word *dusky*? That's what the light was, beautiful and dawnish. We found a spit created by the receding tide. A spit curl, really: it spiraled around. We walked to the end of it. Edward had already removed the screw that kept the wooden urn shut. He took off the lid. The ashes were in a small white container like a film canister. We opened it up, and then we cast the ashes upon the water, hoping they would . . . what? He wouldn't return to us, but we hoped someone would. It was tremendously comforting. Fingertip after fingertip, we let him fly.

It probably sounds ridiculous to observe that I was at that moment already a day or two pregnant, as nearly as I can reckon it. If this morning appeared in a movie, I would spit on it for its nauseating symbolism, the author taking liberties with probability to Give Hope to the Audience. I'm a cynic. I've had to go back to the e-mails I wrote that afternoon, to Ann and Lib and my parents, to make sure that it all really happened.

So: I will report now that when it was done we turned back and walked to the car and passed by the first birder of the morning, a man in his sixties, and his grizzled dog. And that we got in the car and then decided to drive through the miles of parkland around Holkham Hall. We drove through the gates, past the pub we'd liked, and into the grounds.

Then Edward said, "Look!"

Huddled together under a nearby tree were about

thirty does. In my memory they look slightly worried, twisting their heads over their shoulders — to look at us? wondering where everyone else had gone to? All our married life, Edward will say, *Look*, and point, and it will take me several moments: he has spotted the heron, the big brown hare, the cardinal so red it can only be called cardinal red. He grew up in the country. He sees the wildlife. I reflected on this truth as I watched the beautiful kaffeeklatsch of does worry beneath their tree. Then I looked to my right.

My God.

In the wide open, in a dip in the land, were hundreds of deer. *Hundreds*. Fawns, does, stags, everyone, in a giant herd, the stags marshaling the edges.

"Look," I said.

The deer moved around one another. They shifted, but they didn't flee. We could see another car stopped on the other side of the pack, and two people on foot. We bipeds held still.

"I've never seen a stag in the wild before," Edward said. I said, "Well, then."

Finally we drove away. We had to get on the road; it was time for the rest of our lives. On the other side of Holkham Hall, the mawkish entity orchestrating all of this threw in for good measure a clump of stags, fifteen maybe, standing behind a knoll, and when we passed by they ducked down like juvenile delinquents as though to hide. Their antlers still forked up.

I don't believe in omens. Still, it's nice to see Nature try her best to persuade you.

But if you ask me whether this felt like closure, I'll tell you what I've come to believe:

Closure is bullshit.

We were lucky that Edward was standing in the grubby kitchen of our rental house in Saratoga Springs when I came down the stairs with the pregnancy test: we were lucky he was in the United States at all. I suppose I was aware that generally speaking, immigration to the States is no cakewalk. I have seen the movies about green card marriages, but we had been married three years, with pictures to prove it, no quickie job at the courthouse (cheap secular weddings being more suspect), but in fancy dress, with caterers. When we'd lived in the United States before, Edward had gotten short-term visas from the University of Iowa, first as a fellow and then as a teacher. We assumed it would be easy.

It turned out to be very complicated, very fraught, and very boring. Suffice it to say that having applied outside of the country, Edward was supposed to wait until the U.S. government agreed to grant him an immigrant visa. This would take at least six months. The U.S. government, recognizing the difficulty of a long separation, had invented a different kind of visa that would allow a citizen to bring a spouse or fiancé in the meantime. The wait time for that sort of visa was also six months.

In Norfolk I had written letters explaining our case. I called and e-mailed every number and address I could find, explaining why we couldn't bear to be separated come September, when I would have to go to New York to start my job. My father's boss found a lawyer with connections at the INS who helped us for free, but by summer's end the application had made it through only the first of three governmental offices.

Every time I called the American embassy in London for advice, using the pound-a-minute help line, I got a different answer. Finally I was told: it was legal for him to come with me to the United States like any tourist as long as he understood that he'd have to come back to England to get the visa to allow him to go back to America to get his green card. Completely legal. Of course, it was also completely legal for the border official to turn him back immediately if he suspected that Edward had no intention of leaving the country to finish the process.

Edward dressed in his best clothing, bought a necktie at Heathrow, organized all his immigration papers, rehearsed his explanations, bought the round-trip ticket that would take him back to England after ninety days. We flew across the ocean, white-knuckled, hoping for a female agent. Or a sympathetic agent. Or anyone who was not the American equivalent of the man in Portsmouth. At Logan Airport in Boston, I flew through the U.S. Citizens line, then lurked against a wall, watching to see whose booth Edward would end up directed to: the blond man with the brush cut, the dark-haired woman closest to me. He bounced into the woman's lane, and I saw him begin to talk, his shoulders up, his hands explaining. *Don't talk so much!* I thought worriedly, but she had already picked up the stamp that would give him ninety days in the country, and minutes later he was next to me. We grinned and walked to baggage claim as though we didn't care, as though we were being watched and assessed on closed-circuit TV. Now we could start worrying about the next step.

Our first night in the grubby rental house, we lay on an old futon and stared at the acoustic tiles in the ceiling. They reminded me of elementary school classrooms from my 1970s childhood. The combination of Febreze, mothballs, and old cigarette smoke seemed to fill my entire head: I could feel the chemicals muscle their way up my nose and into my skull, which got more packed with every inhalation.

"This can't be good," I said.

I had known I was pregnant again for eight hours. The world felt perilous. In France I'd been kept busy ducking pathogens in food. All raw vegetables are contraindicated by doctors in France, because of the high rate of toxoplasmosis in French soil; nothing is cooked through; you can't count on milk being pasteurized; you are tormented by excellent but forbidden pâtés. Now I was scared of air. Our landlords were elderly and absentee, and when we told the woman they'd hired to look over the house that we needed to hire cleaners, she was dubious. "They had the place professionally cleaned in May," she explained, though it was September. I had taken her on a tour of the filth, and though she couldn't disagree of course she felt accused. "I don't think they'll go for it again."

The next day I took myself to the head of the English Department to ask for advice on what to do about the house.

"You see," I said to Linda, "I'm pregnant again—"

"Oh, Elizabeth!" she burst out. "That's the best possible news!"

I teared up and laughed at the same time. The best possible news! Of course it was! In my state over the house and my general fear, I'd forgotten. For a few months, Linda was the only person besides us who knew I was pregnant. I'd lean into her office and wink, or give the thumbs-up, to tell her that everything was fine. Even after I'd told a few friends, and then our families (we waited till we saw them in person), I didn't go out of my way to tell people. My fantasy was that I'd turn up in a handful of months with a baby. "Oh, this?" I'd say. "This is what I've been working on in my spare time."

All summer long we'd waited for the autopsy results. I wanted to read them and I didn't want to read them: I was terrified that the verdict would say, essentially, *Cause of death: maternal oblivion.*

The report had finally shown up after a small international dance of paperwork. Using the Internet I could decipher the conclusion: chorioamniotitis, with no known histological cause. Lib knew a French-speaking doctor who spent an hour with me on the phone. The report had two halves. The first was about me, the blood tests they'd run, the umbilical cord and placenta and uterus. Olivier went through in a very calm voice, translating and then explaining the medical terms. There was some inflammation to the cord, and some dead spots on the placenta, but it was impossible to know whether these had caused Pudding's death, or whether his death had resulted in them. I'd scanned the second half, which was entirely about his body, its perfection, its blamelessness. You couldn't blame his kidneys. His heart was faultless.

"It doesn't look like we need to go through that," said Olivier. He'd been wonderful, calm, warm. "We could—"

"No," I said. "Let's not."

"No," he agreed, and I could hear the relief in his voice.

The midwives had said that the umbilical cord was looped around his neck and that the amniotic fluid was low, but we'll never know what happened. I'm fine with that. No one explanation, no one moment I can worry over, rub at in my brain, saying, *There. If only I'd done exactly that differently.*

Still, pregnant for the second time, some days I just imagined that I had done everything wrong, and was doing everything wrong all over again. All chemicals seemed dangerous; ditto substances organic and dirty. Mothballs, mice, Febreze, mold, lead dust, flies—baby killers, every last one.

Anyhow, one of my kind and eloquent colleagues talked to the landlords, and they agreed to hire professional cleaners, and that was that.

No, I insist: other people's children did not make me sad. But pregnant women did. In the waiting room of a Saratoga Springs ob-gyn practice, for my first visit, I watched the other women. The practice was next to Saratoga Hospital, which we could see from the back windows of the grubby rental house. One woman had brought a toddler boy, who held in his lap a plastic toy that played "The Wheels on the Bus" in a doorbell-to-hell electronic chime. A younger woman tugged at her low-slung maternity jeans as she backed into a chair, and then she patted her stomach. "When are you due?" asked the already mother, and the young woman answered, "Friday. I can't wait." *I have nothing in common with you,* I thought. That shows I had already forgotten the one lesson I'd vowed to learn: you can never guess at the complicated history of strangers.

All of a sudden I missed Savary, missed being the only woman in an unwed mothers' home: I wanted to go away with Edward and not mention anything to anyone until we had an actual baby to show off. *If* we had an actual baby to show off. The waiting room end tables were piled high with pregnancy and parenting magazines, every one as sweet and awful and toxic as the Febreze-scented curtains back at the house. And then *I* felt toxic, outgassing pessimism, worry, bad luck.

Even the paperwork was intolerable. I checked boxes and wrote terse explanations. *Previous pregnancies:* 1. *Living children:* 0. *Explanation* . . . The receptionists were being raucous behind the glass window into their office, but when the young woman took my clipboard and reviewed it she looked up at me, full of sympathy.

I sat back down and flipped through the stacks of magazines until I found a copy of *O,* with a cheerful, childless Oprah Winfrey on the front. Then the nurse called me in.

First the familiar urine sample. I carried the half-filled cup, as directed, down the hall to a far examining room, which was disconcertingly decorated with wood paneling and pheasant-patterned wallpaper and pheasant-themed prints. The doctor was a man in his fifties; the office was his. It felt like the den of a befuddled father of many daughters, the place he went for a little manly time alone with his pheasantalia, only to discover that no matter what, he was chased by damnable women who insisted on offering him cups of urine before dropping their pants. He flipped through my just completed records.

"This is your first pregnancy?" he asked. If I hadn't become pregnant again, I might have gone years without saying it. This was the first time of many; I'd say it every month, then every week, then twice a week. "I had a child who was stillborn."

The doctor was pleasant and kindly, but he seemed unsure of how to respond. Medically, I'm sure he did know, but personally he seemed uncomfortable, and who could blame him? Some things can't be reduced to their medical facts. He cleared his throat. "Any postpartum depression with the last pregnancy?"

"Well," I said. "Well."

He nodded and turned back to his paperwork.

At the end of that first appointment I had to schedule the next. "Who do you want?" the receptionist asked. "Doctor? Midwife?"

"Doctor," I said. "If that's all right." I didn't blame midwifery for Pudding's death, I just couldn't bear the idea of too much warmth from a medical professional. All my romantic notions about collaborating on a birth had gone out the window. I wanted to be told what to do; I swore I would obey.

Besides, what were the chances?

When I returned for every successive appointment, the pregnant women in the waiting room made me sad: there they sat in the present, dreaming of the future. I couldn't bear watching. I wanted a separate waiting room for people like me, with different magazines. No *Parenting* or *Wondertime* or *Pregnancy,* no ads with pink or tawny or pearly smiling infants. I wanted *Hold Your Horses Magazine. Don't Count Your Chickens for Women. Pregnant for the Time Being Monthly.* Here I was, only in this second, and then the next, and nothing else. No due dates, no conversations about "the baby" or what life would be like months from now. No "This time will be different" or "Listen, it will all be worth it when you hold your child in your arms." What I wanted, scrawled across my chart in shaky physician's cursive: *NOTE: do not blow sunshine up patient's ass.*

I rotated through the doctors, and they all seemed perfectly capable. In the unlikely event (my God, how we strived to ever lower our expectations) that I actually had a baby, any one of them would be welcome to extract it.

And then I had an appointment with Dr. Knoeller.

Almost immediately Edward and I took to calling Dr. Knoeller "Bones," because she was a doctor (short for Sawbones, like the doctor on *Star Trek*) and because she was extraordinarily thin, but mostly, I think, because we instantly worshipped the ground she walked on and it helped us to be irreverent about one small thing. The appointment was our last checkup of my first trimester, and she looked at the chart.

"Is this your first child?"

"I had a stillbirth last year," I said.

"I'm so sorry," she said immediately, words I've never tired of hearing. We went over the details a little, and then she said, "You've scheduled an amnio."

"Yes," I said. In France the blond Baltimorean asked us

if we were worriers; when we said yes, she made an appointment for an amniocentesis. Even so, I'd been startled when I spoke to the French genetic counselor, who was heavily pregnant herself, and she informed me that if the results came back positive for Down syndrome, they "recommended" that we terminate the pregnancy. Edward and I hadn't discussed what we'd do if it turned out that Pudding had Down syndrome, because we agreed that all the theorizing in the world would probably crumble to dust in the face of a fact.

But this time it was different. We simply wanted to know. It would only be information.

"I mean," I said to Dr. Knoeller, "we figured we might as well. I guess. I don't know. What do you think?"

Well, she said, the real question was, if we had an amnio, and the results were normal, but it was one of the one in two hundred pregnancies that miscarried after the procedure, how would we feel?

We were stunned into silence, because of course that was the question. Even if you rephrased it — as Edward pointed out, one in two hundred sounds worse than one half of one percent because with the former you visualize actual people — we weren't willing to risk it. Once you've been on the losing side of great odds, you never find statistics comforting again.

She said in a manner both businesslike and warm, "Let me just say that I had an amnio myself, but I didn't have your history."

And just like that, our history was in the room, and I had found a doctor I loved.

Another woman might want a doctor who promised things: an optimist, a dreamer. Not me. I wanted exact realism and no promises. On one visit a nurse spoke of the kid as though he or she was a foregone conclusion, and I hated it, I wanted to correct her, I wanted to point out that I'd thought that once, and look what happened.

"Well, very good," Dr. Knoeller said at the end of every visit. "So far, so good. Let's hope it continues that way."

And then I was twenty-eight weeks pregnant, and when Dr. Knoeller walked into the room, I swore you could see Walt Disney bluebirds toying with her stethoscope and bunnies congregating around her heels.

"Twenty-eight weeks!" she said. "Now we can relax."

For my first pregnancy I couldn't imagine not finding out the baby's gender. I'd asked Lib why she'd allowed her two daughters to keep their mystery in utero, and she said, "I didn't want to project who I thought they'd be. I wanted them to be themselves."

This is exactly the kind of thoughtful and maternal answer I'd expected from Lib. Me, I *wanted* to project. I was impatient to make up stories about whoever Pudding was, kicking about in my midsection, but how could I without that essential piece of information? For our second child we decided to do everything differently — no amnio, no peeking during ultrasounds. Now and then I wondered whether that was wise: should something happen (it won't!), should the worst happen (it's not impossible!), wouldn't we rather know? It's terrible to miss Pudding, of course, no matter what, but — this is a total illusion, I understand, nothing but the sentimentality of expectant parents spinning fairy tales ahead of time, viewed in the rearview mirror—it feels like we *knew* him. I can't wrap my brain around losing a child and learning only then whether you'd lost a son or a daughter. Not finding out felt like an odd form of optimism.

By the end of my first pregnancy I'd felt very tender toward Pudding—to my made-up companionable Pudding, an infant who would of course love us the minute he saw us, who loved us already, who contained within him not only infancy but babyhood and toddlerhood, who already listened to our voices, who was impatient to meet us (so why was he taking his time?). I stroked my stomach and told him stories; when he kicked, I poked him back. We went to the pool together, me swimming in the chlorinated municipal water of Bergerac, he swimming inside me, both incredulous at how the French could gossip while doing the backstroke. We went to the gym together, where the French not only gossiped and kissed each other in the squat rack, but tucked their shirts into their exercise pants. I ate so that he could eat: I announced what was on the menu.

You don't need much to hang a personality on someone you haven't met: a name, some knowledge of the parents, a gender. You can spin anything you want out of those things.

But it wasn't all so easy. Every now and then, like any pregnant woman, I would panic. *When did I last feel this baby move?* Then I would lie on the sofa, and put my hands on my stomach, and wait to feel a kick, and then another. Both Dr. Baltimore and Dr. Bergerac had sonograms in their offices, and so for the first six months we saw Pudding on the Big Screen every month. Yes, I did worry, sometimes.

But mostly I didn't.

This is one of the most painful things for me to remember. I was smug. I felt sorry for women with complicated pregnancies and gloated that I wasn't one of them. I believed that the pregnancy would continue to be a delight. I imagined that traveling with him afterward, at four weeks old, to England and then to America, would be only an adventure, a story I would tell him for the rest of his life.

I believed he was perfect.

I don't know whether my faith is explained by hormones or misplaced trust in medical science. I just believed he was perfect. I believed I understood him.

Of course that wasn't true of my second pregnancy, when I was certain every other moment that something was going terribly wrong. I was neurotic about food; I washed my hands like an insane person. Among my many worries was that I would feel unconnected to this second occupant and that this indifference would travel through the placenta and warp the developing psyche. But I turned out to feel another sort of closeness. Pregnant with Pudding, I often didn't even realize how big I'd gotten; we communicated via dream telegraph. During my second pregnancy, I was by necessity obsessed with the physical, and this baby—who was in there, anyhow?—was a great in utero kicker and squirmer. Once the kid was big enough for me to feel, I would think once a day, panicked, *When's the last time I felt the baby move?* And then I'd palm my stomach. Thump, thump, thump. What a good baby, what a wonderful obliging baby, was there something *wrong* with that baby, to make it shift so? Was that a kick or a shudder or head banging? You couldn't deny it: there was a baby in there. Even so, I sometimes wondered whether I was making it up.

"Shh," I'd say to my stomach, "you're all right," and to Edward, "Who's in there, do you think? It could be *anyone.*"

"Not *anyone,*" he'd say, looking a little troubled.

I taught my classes and grew subtly stouter but said nothing. It seemed as though something terrible would happen if people knew. By which I mean: not that we would be tempting fate, but that I would have to acknowledge that the pregnancy was real, and if I did that, I was sure, I would take to my bed until spring. I told a handful of friends in October, and a handful of relatives at Thanksgiving.

Lib insisted I was having a girl. Edward, who had correctly and with great certainty predicted Pudding's gender, agreed. I had no idea. When I was four months in, Ann declared, no room for argument, that I was pregnant with a boy, and listen: her husband's daughter was pregnant, too, and Ann had said Josephine was going to have a boy, and the first ultrasound had the temerity to disagree with Ann's prediction, but Ann wouldn't budge, and then the second ultrasound said, All right, yes, a boy.

This perturbed Edward. "I thought I knew," he said. "Why'd Ann have to say that?"

At the hardware store a woman behind the counter said, "So do you know for sure you're having a boy?" but a pedicurist the same day shook her head and said, Girl, and wasn't a pedicurist almost a medical professional? It amused me to spend so much time pondering a question that could be at any time answered with reasonable certainty. By the last month of pregnancy I had my amniotic fluid checked by ultrasound twice weekly, not to mention plenty of other diagnostic tools. But I never bent.

Maybe I had just acquired new superstitions, and given them disguises.

W e'd planned for Pudding in stories, plane tickets to see family, and tiny French outfits. Then I was pregnant again and we counted on nothing, and so we prepared for the future by taking classes. We signed up for four:

1. A four-week childbirth class through my ob-gyn practice, taught by one of my favorite people there, the nurse coordinator. Of course I already knew what to expect of such a class. I watched TV, didn't I? We'd sit on the floor in the bobsled position, surrounded by other couples, and Edward would be told to tell me to breathe.

We never left our chairs, and in fact we knew most of what was taught, having been through childbirth before. I wanted to raise my hand and interrupt the lovely nurse every other sentence to say: "You mean *if,* not when."

2. An infant car seat installation class. We were the only ones who showed up. The instructor was a thin blond

woman, I think in her late forties, who had four sons, aged four, seven, seventeen, and twenty-five. I was dying to know her story, but I didn't ask. Her teaching style appealed to us, because like auto safety professionals everywhere her message was: YOU COULD EASILY GET DECAPITATED OR DECAPITATE SOMEONE ELSE! But! DECAPITATION IS EASY TO PREVENT IF YOU AREN'T DUMB AND CARELESS LIKE THE REST OF THE WORLD. The worst could happen, here's how to minimize it. That's what we wanted.

We started the class with a short test, which included the question "What is an accident?"

The answer she was looking for: an accident is force times mass. That is, she wanted to impress upon us that in an accident, loose objects in the car — water bottles, spare change, and so forth — could become imbedded in, or pass through, your child. Everything should be locked in the trunk, though purses were fine as long as they were zipped shut and seat-belted in.

We'd already had our seat installed at the local firehouse by two policemen who'd struggled with the job. One had the sort of authoritative, well-tended mustache that only police or firemen can carry off; the other was tall and curly-haired. Together they crawled into the backseat of our car and frowned. "This is a hard car," one had said, and I theorized that the Cadillac Catera — my parents had given it to us when they'd bought a new

Subaru — had not been designed for the childbearing demographic. The policemen pushed and pulled and used a wedge of foam noodles duct-taped together, and then, as they showed us how to buckle a baby doll into the removable seat, told us not to move the base if we could avoid it. We told them we were taking a class in a few days, but we wouldn't let the teacher move it. "You're taking a class with Cindy?" one of the policemen said. He looked frankly a little frightened.

Cindy, it turned out, had taught the policemen how to install seats, and she was skeptical about the foam noodles. "Right," she said. "Let's see what one woman can accomplish compared to two men." In three minutes she'd reinstalled the seat without the noodles, and then she taught Edward.

"Can I keep this?" she asked, slapping her palm with the noodle wedge like an old-fashioned movie policeman with his nightstick. "I'm going to see those guys next week at a safety event, and I'd like to give them this as a present."

3. An infant care class at the local hospital. In truth, neither Edward nor I knew anything about babies. Surely most of it was on-the-job training, but some advice on, say, diaper changing and bathing would help. For the first three hours of this session, the labor and delivery nurse who taught it explained the various things that could make your newborn baby look unsightly — stork bites; tarry black stool; rashes of all kinds; thick, greasy,

channel-swimming fat; back hair; lumps from vacuum deliveries; dents from forceps deliveries.

Then we got on the issue of circumcision.

Perhaps the only real conversation Edward and I have ever had on the subject of religion came after our wedding. We'd been married with dueling officiants, now the village priest and his sonorous voice and official vows, now the American rabbi and the smashed glass and cries of mazel tov. I had been late to the service. To fill time, the church organist played first "If I Were a Rich Man" and then "Jesus Christ Superstar." In other words, it had taken some work to appeal to both of our families.

"My mother says the next thing to worry about is christenings and circumcisions," I said to him.

"No to both," he said, and we solemnly shook hands on it.

So I didn't say anything at all about it when the topic came up: we knew what we'd do. The nurse, who'd already distinguished herself by saying that the administration of eye salve was mandated in "all forty-eight states," was clearly completely and totally against circumcision but knew that she couldn't say so. Well, not in so many words. "The United States," she said, "is the only so-called civilized country that regularly circumcises. So think about that."

"It seems," said one thoughtful young husband, "like a lot of people say that you should circumcise a boy so he'll look like his father."

"Yes!" said the nurse. "And you know what? How

many men are homophobic? Let's face it: all of them! So what are the chances you'll be hanging around naked with your kid anyhow?"

Apparently I made a noise that was translatable as: lady, that is eighteen kinds of batshit.

"You don't agree?" she asked me.

Now I should say I'd already gotten in trouble because she'd earlier heard me making fun of the swaddled infant she'd drawn on the whiteboard. Also, when she'd said the thing about forty-eight states, I'd turned to Edward, and said, "That's not right," just so that he, a foreigner, would not be confused, I swear that's the only reason.

What I'm saying is I was already not Nurse Batshit's favorite student.

"Well," I stuttered, "I mean, I don't know, it's not, it's just, I don't think — listen, you don't need to convince me anyhow: I'm married to a European."

"I have a European parent," she said, in a voice that suggested that I meant *European* to be a euphemism for *nudist:* she understood, but this really wasn't the place to discuss it.

I'm glad I wasn't being graded.

4. An infant CPR class. This took place in the basement of the public library and was the most oversubscribed class of all, as well as the most motley: there were two other heavily pregnant women, a bunch of day care workers, a few other couples, and some EMTs brushing up on their skills. The teacher was a pepper pot of a woman

with six kids. She'd brought two of them with her, a pair of mismatched nine-year-old fraternal twin boys.

The rescue mannequins were the usual beige objects that looked as though they'd died of heroin overdoses, even the two infant dummies. There weren't enough to go around, so to make up for the lack, the teacher had brought a variety of dolls. For instance, Elmo. And Kermit the Frog. And the green Teletubby, the Cat in the Hat, a Rugrat, a character I'd never heard of called Doug, Raggedy Ann, and a Cabbage Patch doll. The history of beloved commercial dolls. She gave us pieces of plastic to lay over the mouths—or muzzles, or whatever you call the thing through which a Teletubby takes its nourishment—dental dams, essentially, to make safe the practice of artificial respiration on toys. The man next to us had the green Teletubby. He was the only person there who was learning for a specific, already earthbound person: his son, he said happily in a Chinese accent as thick as his crew cut, was five days old. You would have easily picked him out as the new father, he was so tender with the Teletubby, so cautious as he supported its head and adjusted the bit of plastic wrap.

The twins stood in when we learned about older children.

"Here's where you press," the instructor said, indicating the spot on the littler twin. He had blond ringlets and a potbelly.

"And then they throw up!" he said.

"Yes, sometimes," she said.

"And then they *eat* it!"

"That doesn't happen," his mother said, frowning.

"Who wants to save me?" the taller twin asked the students politely, but we were all a little shy about rescuing a perfectly safe boy, right in sight of his mother.

I made sure I got my hands on one of the actual dummies, the kind with a balloon down its throat, whose chest rose when you blew into the mouth: I needed the physical reassurance. I put my hand across its torso. As long as I breathed, the dying plastic baby breathed. When I stopped, it stopped.

"Listen," the woman announced suddenly, in the voice I recognized from fourth grade, a room full of kids working on projects, a teacher with a point: *listen up, people.* "Listen, children don't die. They rarely die."

She said this to calm us. If you think that children rarely die, then it's easier to save them. I dandled the plastic baby on my knee and bit my lip.

My notes from that class say:

WORRY IN THIS ORDER
A ir
B reathing
C irculation

And that of course is why we were taking all those courses: We wanted to be told, Worry in this order. We were delighted to know the damage a single loose almond in the cab of a car could do in the event of an accident, because then we could remove that almond and be vigilant about future dropped almonds. We wanted to hear all the details of a caesarean just in case; we wanted to know ahead of time how common vacuum-assisted births were. Once, we had belonged to the school of Cross That Bridge When We Come to It. Now we wanted all bridges mapped, the safety of their struts, their likelihood of washing out, their vulnerability to blackguards, angry natives, cougars.

H ere is the worst thing that happened during my second pregnancy.

Edward had gone back to England for a month so that he could come back to America. I went to the doctor because I was worried about some minor pregnancy symptom. The ob-gyn was a nice bespectacled woman in her fifties, who I'd never seen before. Earlier in the pregnancy a different doctor had said, "Now, this is just about the time when you can hear a heartbeat," and she'd put the monitor on my stomach and found nothing and we'd been rushed into the sonogram room, where all was well. Now, weeks later, the bespectacled doctor could not find a heartbeat.

At first that was fine. I lay back and let her feel around and remembered the earlier impossible-to-find heartbeat.

"There it is!" the bespectacled doctor said, and then "No, that's you." She took hold of my wrist to feel my pulse, slower than a baby's. Every now and then we heard a thud

thud through the monitor, and she'd pincer my wrist and shake her head: me again. *I* had a heartbeat.

After a while, I thought, Well. What if this is it? What do I do next? Call Edward in England, of course, but then what? Do I go home and get drunk? Drive like hell in the direction of my nearest good friend? Throw myself into the Hudson?

She said, "It's no good. Now your heart is beating so fast, I won't be able to tell the difference."

I was rushed to the sonogram room. "Yup, there," said the beautiful sonographer, nodding at the screen. Her name was Barb, and I loved her. The bespectacled doctor (who of course knew my history from my chart) put her hands on her head and walked in the several small circles of relief that Edward would have completed if he were there.

Poor woman. She'd been panicking as much as I had.

P erhaps it goes without saying that I believe in the geographic cure. Of course you can't out-travel sadness. You will find it has smuggled itself along in your suitcase. It coats the camera lens, it flavors the local cuisine. In that different sunlight, it stands out, awkward, yours, honking in the brash vowels of your native tongue in otherwise quiet restaurants. You may even feel proud of its stubbornness as it follows you up the bell towers and monuments, as it pants in your ear while you take in the view. I travel not to get away from my troubles but to see how they look in front of famous buildings or on deserted beaches. I take them for walks. Sometimes I get them drunk. Back at home we generally understand each other better.

So at the end of February, when I was seven months pregnant, we took the train from Albany to New Orleans, where I'd been invited to give a reading. Saratoga Springs was still packed in graying snow, left over from a Valen-

tine's Day blizzard, and my pregnancy was no longer a secret from strangers, who cooed over my stomach, and said,
"First child? You must be so excited!" We booked a tiny
room with folding bunk beds for the train ride — the very
definition of hell for some people, I know, but it was fan-
tastic. Our across-the-corridor neighbor was an elderly
English Franciscan monk and train buff, exactly the sort of
person you can get to know only on a long train trip. We
took all of our lousy, happy Amtrak meals with him.

In Tuscaloosa, at a pause, we stepped onto the platform
and sniffed at the sunrise. We were riding into spring. This
visit had originally been planned in the innocent April of
2005, for that October, when I would have been three
months pregnant with Pudding. In Paris, just after the
Gulf Coast's calamity, I had to explain it to the beautiful
woman in the Air France office near the Jardins du Lux-
embourg: New Orleans was under water. Everything was
canceled. She smiled sympathetically but would not refund
the ticket. The college asked me again for the spring of
2006, but I had to write back with my regrets: I planned to
be heavily pregnant or giving birth for the entire spring.

What would it be like, postdiluvian us in postdiluvian
New Orleans?

On our first full day our hostess took us on what she
called the Devastation Tour of the city: the haunted Lower
Ninth Ward, where one woman stood on the porch of the
only renovated house for blocks, her moving van parked
out front. We saw the house of the filmmaker Helen Hill,

who'd been shot to death by an intruder while her husband scooped up their baby and ran to safety; we looked at some levees, which seemed to have been stapled back together and left to rust; we passed by other people on similar tours. Everywhere you could see protoplasmic high-water marks on houses, some low enough that you'd know that only the things in the basement were ruined, some so high you wondered how it was that the entire neighborhood had not been washed away. Other houses still had the international orange tattoos left after the storm: date searched; number of people saved; number of people who, being dead, were merely discovered. We ended up at the new Whole Foods near the studio apartment that had been rented for us, goggle-eyed at all that disorienting bounty. Who would need to buy, in such a world, a precooked vegan meatloaf?

"I don't think they're done finding bodies," our hostess told us. She'd just gone on antianxiety medication so that she could bear living in the city she loved.

Spring had arrived just ahead of us, in the form of actual blossoms — magnolias — and the weird kudzu of flung-from-floats Mardi Gras beads in the trees. The city was all blue skies and light breezes and raw nerves and melancholy. Most everyone we met was on edge, some so heartsick we worried, even if we'd never met them before. They seemed frozen. Something had happened. It had been a year and a half, and if you weren't in the middle of it you might lose patience: New Orleans, why can't you get over it? We were very sorry for you for a while. Now there are other things to be sad about. It's not your time anymore. Pull yourself together.

Of course it felt familiar, as wretchedly presumptuous as that sounds. I'd spent the fall and winter feeling only the most cautious of emotions. A gleam of hope, a spike of fear, slantwise guilty grief. One day's worth of feeling at a time. Surely grand emotion is more than twenty-four hours' worth, grief compounded with interest, joy magnified by anticipated returns. In New Orleans, I found it extraordinary to be surrounded by great sadness. The people we saw, old friends and strangers, had left and come back, and now they were waiting for the next disaster, the next murder, the next hurricane, the next levee failure, the loss of their home, the revocation of their homeowner's insurance, and still of course at the same time they had to hope. Hadn't they come back for that reason, because they hoped?

Me, too: same place, remembering the disaster, trying to believe it would not come for me again.

At a reception that week, I was chatting with the exceptionally lovely, soft-spoken woman who'd donated the money for the program that had brought me there. We sat in folding chairs against a wall, a few feet from the buffet table. Just small talk. She asked me how my pregnancy was going. Then she said, "I was so sorry when I heard about your first child. My first child was stillborn, too."

My heart kicked on like a furnace. Suddenly tears were pouring down my face.

"Oh no!" said the woman. "I didn't mean for that to happen!"

I laughed and grabbed some napkins from the table and tried to explain myself, though even now it's hard to find the words. What came over me was gratitude and an entirely inappropriate love. I didn't know the woman, but I loved her. I'd felt the same thing meeting another couple on campus, a professor and his wife who'd written me when Pudding died to send condolences and to say that they'd had a daughter who was stillborn nearly thirty years before.

All I can say is, it's a sort of kinship, as though there is a family tree of grief. On this branch the lost children, on this the suicided parents, here the beloved mentally ill siblings. When something terrible happens, you discover all of a sudden that you have a new set of relatives, people with whom you can speak in the shorthand of cousins.

Twice now I have heard the story of someone who knows someone who's had a stillborn child since Pudding has died, and it's all I can do not to book a flight immediately, to show up somewhere I'm not wanted, just so that I can say, *It happened to me, too,* because it meant so much to me to hear it. *It happened to me, too,* meant: *It's not your fault.* And *You are not a freak of nature.* And *This does not have to be a secret.*

That's how it works. When a baby dies, other dead children become suddenly visible: Daughters and sons. First cousins. The neighbor kid. The first child. The last child.

Your older brother. Some of their names have been forgotten; some never had names in the first place. They disappeared under heaps of advice. Don't dwell. Have another child, a makeup baby. Life is for the living. But then another baby dies, and here they are again, in stories, and you will love them all, and — if you are the mother of a dead child yourself — they will keep coming to you. *A couple I know just lost their baby.* And you will know that your lost child has appeared somewhere else in the world. *I know a couple . . .*

All those dead children. Who knows what they want?

In our better moments, we surely understand that the dead do not need anything. Afterlife, no afterlife: the dead have their needs taken care of. Oh, but isn't wanting things something else again, and don't we talk about it all the time. *It's what he would have wanted. Her last wishes.* Thank God for the dead; thank God someone is capable of making a decision in the worst of times: *He would have liked it that way.*

But a baby. Who's to say? Babies are born needing everything. They're a state of emergency. That's what they're for. Dead, there's nothing we can do for them, and we don't know what they'd want, we can't even guess. I can pretend that I knew Pudding. No, I did know him, not with my brain but with my body, and yet I know nothing about him, not even the simplest thing: I have no idea of what he'd want. And so in my grief I understand that mourning is a kind of ventriloquism; we put words into the mouths of our bereavers, but of course it's all entirely about us, our wants, our needs, the dead are satisfied, we are greedy, greedy, greedy, unseemly, self-obsessed. If your child did not survive his birth, everyone can see that clearly. I want. I need. Not him. No pretending.

I thought stillbirth was a thing of history, and then it happened to me, and yet now when I hear of a baby dying I'm just as incredulous. *You mean they* still *haven't figured this out?* I want to hear about every dead baby, everywhere in the world. I want to know their names, Christopher, Strick, Jonathan. I want their mothers to know about Pudding.

The dead don't need anything. The rest of us could use some company.

When I was about thirty-six weeks pregnant the second time, Edward mentioned that his grandmother had been named Mabel. I'd known this, of course, but forgotten.

"Mabel," I said. "Mabel. Mabel!"

We'd scarcely discussed names at all. In the back of our heads, we remembered the boy names we'd come up with for Pudding, both of us leaning toward the names we'd rejected early in the process, like Moses and George. For five minutes we'd discussed girl names and come up with Lucy, Beatrix, and Penelope. That was all we could manage. We didn't joke about names the way we had the first time — Fatty Harvey, Phineas T. Harvey, Charles Laughton Harvey. We didn't joke much at all. All of the jokes we'd made when I was pregnant with Pudding had to be retired, and it was hard to come up with new ones.

But now *Mabel* was in my head, and I was a little in love with it. I called Ann and Lib and got their reactions. (They loved it, or at least said they did. Lib declared that she would call our baby Mabel no matter the gender.) *Mabel,* I thought. I pictured a little girl named Mabel — not necessarily our little girl named Mabel, but an ordinary everyday Mabel. You had to love a little girl named Mabel. I hadn't felt this way about any of the other little-girl names. I'd never felt this about any of the little-boy names of a year before, not even my favorite of the lot: Oscar. Sometimes I said to Edward, in a voice full of meaning, "Mabel."

"Maybe," he said.

I rubbed my stomach. "Mabel?" I said. "Do I love 'Mabel' because you're a Mabel?"

Thump thump, went the obliging, enigmatic baby.

Over the past year and over my second pregnancy, of course I thought about Pudding all the time, every day, possibly every waking hour. (It's possible I still do think of him every waking hour, and if I were the kind of new mother who kept track of things — diapers, feedings, naps — I could mark down *thoughts of first child* as well.) But mostly I didn't think about the details of his death. If I climbed into that pit, I'd never crawl out, I'd have been at the ob-gyn practice every single day, begging Dr. Knoeller for an ultrasound, a sedative, an emergency C-section. I wasn't counting my chickens, this one chicken, this essential chicken — but I wasn't imagining heart-stopping scenarios, either.

Then it was early April.

Then it was mid-April.

I'm not a fool. I could see the end of April coming toward me. We'd known all along I'd be induced, and I'd said that I wanted to avoid the end of April, particularly

April 27, not for my own sake but for the kid's: it seemed like a too weighty fact to have in your biography, being born a year to the day after your brother who didn't survive, the sort of thing I wouldn't countenance in a modern novel. And then I said, Who cares, I don't care, whatever happens, I'll accept it. Dr. Knoeller had already suggested May 2, when I would be thirty-eight weeks and two days pregnant and she would be on call. But as she pointed out, I could go into labor before that.

Is it melodramatic to say that for the month of April, I was heavy with two children? There was the child in front of me, of course. Twice a week I went for monitoring, first fetal heartbeat and responsiveness, then amniotic fluid. Once a week we went to see Dr. Knoeller. All the signs looked very good.

But Pudding was with me then, and stronger than ever. Fifty-two weeks before, I'd walked the roads near Savary, hoping to trigger labor. Fifty-one weeks before, I'd sat in Bordeaux cafés, crying. I had been sad for nearly a year, but I had *gone forward*. That had been our plan all along. "We can only go forward," Edward had said a dozen times, two dozen, all through our Holt summer, and every time I made the merest noise of wondering how it might have turned out otherwise, he would say lovingly, firmly, "Sweetheart, don't." He was right, of course. Blame is a compulsive behavior, the emotional version of obsessive hand washing, until all you can do is hold your palms out till your hands are full of it, and rub, and rub, and accomplish nothing at all. And so we grieved but looked straight ahead.

And then—did I mention this?—it was April again, and I was pregnant again, and there were so many ways, it seemed, that disaster could strike, and nearly though not quite as many ways it could be averted. My hips ached the way they had the year before. I had trouble turning over in bed the way I had. People said, Any day now! And, Have you had that baby yet? On April 30, I had my first real crisis of faith. "This baby isn't moving," I told Edward, and I called the practice, and they told me to come in, and the nurses rushed me into the examination room, and everything was fine.

Dr. Knoeller ran into us in the hall.

"I sort of freaked out," I said, and she said, "If this is the first time, I think you've done very, very well."

It was almost May. I wanted to get through it, and I wanted to remember.

On April 26, 2006, a week after my American due date, Edward asked me, as he often did, "What's Pudding up to?"

"He's not moving around so much," I said. I touched my stomach. I was sitting in Savary's weird L-shaped dining room, next to the only phone outlet in the entire enormous house, so I could check my e-mail. Every now and then, I felt a dim stirring.

"Really?" he said.

"I don't know," I said. Everything I read said that babies move less when they're getting ready to be born: they have less room.

"Should we call someone?" he asked.

And there it is: the first moment I can look at and say, we could have changed things. This is the moment that Superman flies in and puts his hand on the fender of the runaway car to let the child in his cloth coat go toddling into the road after the bright kicked ball.

"No," I said. "Let's wait till morning."

The only reason that writing about this moment doesn't make me weep so hard I can't type is that it's just one of a dozen.

The next morning I lay in bed with my hands on my stomach and then phoned the local fox-faced midwife. As usual, I got her cell phone's voicemail. She called back a few minutes later.

"Could I come in and see you?" I asked. "The baby's not moving as much as he was."

Yes, she said, that happened. But all right. She had many appointments, but at about five —

"Claudelle," I said, "I'm really worried," and I hadn't realized until I said it how worried I was. For some women — me, for instance, during my second pregnancy — hyperworry is a side effect, as sure as high blood pressure or high blood sugar. Your body just produces *more*, which means you do what you can to manage it. But back then when the worry flooded in, I believed it was serious, because it was anomalous.

"All right," she said. "Come now."

Claudelle's waiting room was a glassed-in porch at the back of the house, outside of her office. We had waited there for plenty of appointments, looking over the back fence at the house next door. This time we sat on the wicker sofa for a few minutes, fretting.

She pulled back the curtain over the window in the door,

saw us, and waved us in. Her office was decorated in the sort of filmy orange and blue color scheme that acknowledges you might wish to be elsewhere. Her examining table was stirrupless, massage-worthy. The only overtly medical object in her room was an old-fashioned black doctor's bag, the kind carried by Norman Rockwell GPs. From this, that Thursday morning, she extracted a fetal heart monitor, to give me what is called in America a nonstress test.

This is of course a contradiction in terms, because listening to anyone's heartbeat for half an hour is stressful: it changes, and you want to ask the medical professional, Is that all right? Too fast, too slow? The suspense is terrible. Nonstress just means the heart rate and uterine contractions (if any) are monitored to see how the baby is reacting to normal life in the womb without the added stress of medication to mimic contractions. I'd had a routine nonstress test the week before, when Sylvie, the other midwife, had come to the house.

"There he is!" said Claudelle now, having found the heartbeat.

We'd heard plenty of different monitors by then: the wuAHwuAHwuAH of a silver flying saucer sailing to earth in a 1950s sci-fi movie, a ponyish clippety-clop, an expressionless chain of beeps. Claudelle's usual heart monitor, the one she held to my stomach for uneventful checkups, was horsey, but this one sounded like the forlorn footsteps of a tiny man, walking around a series of corridors, looking for a door. Tok tok tok tok. She pulled at the strap that held the device to try to get closer but couldn't. In my memory the heartbeat got louder and quieter — the tiny man turned a corner, tried a knob, retraced his steps — but that doesn't make sense. Pudding was still alive then, but he probably wasn't moving.

I lay on my side. When Sylvie had tested me the week beforehand, she'd given me a button on a cable to press when I felt Pudding move, but this time I just kept still and listened. The machine spit out a pen-etched tape, like a polygraph result in the movies. Claudelle studied it.

She was perfectly cheerful, she chatted to calm us down. It even worked for a while. Then she put one hand on either side of my stomach and shook. "Hello," she said. "Bonjour, bébé. Wake up. Come, stop sleeping."

Tok, tok, tok, tok.

She shook harder. "Wake up, baby," she said.

After forty-five minutes, she took off the monitor.

"So?" I said.

"So," she said. "I wish he would respond more, but it is not serious."

When I was pregnant the second time, I became an old hand at nonstress tests: I had them twice a week, and mostly they passed without incident. To pass the test, you need four heart rate accelerations within twenty minutes, and I usually hit that mark within ten. The nurses praised the kid for being agreeable, for never needing to be yelled at or jolted into action with fruit juice, though one of the nurses did once slap me around the midsection. "Child abuse, and the kid's not even born," she said, as the heart rate sped up. "Ah, there he goes."

At one of my last tests, I asked the nurse on duty, a sweet young woman with a gamine haircut and a two-year-old of her own, what happened if you failed a nonstress test.

"They'd keep you on for forty minutes," she said, "to make sure the baby's not just sleeping."

And then? I asked.

"Well," she said, "they'd send you to the hospital immediately."

And then? I wondered, but didn't ask.

This is the real Superman moment for me, as I sit at my computer, telling this story. I want to reach into the screen. I want to hit Return between *I wish he would respond more* and *but it is not serious.*

I wish he would respond more —

Look at that lovely white space! There's my laptop screen in front of me. Surely I should be able to touch the space, I am a science-fiction heroine now, touch the space and pull it open. Can't I stretch time if I just push these paragraphs apart? Above, she is saying, *I wish he would respond more.*

In the new bright hole in the computer screen, which is to say, the universe, she then says,

I think you should go to the hospital immediately.

But you cannot. You cannot. You cannot change time. You can't even know that it would have made any difference: a baby can be born alive and still die. A baby can be born sick, and get sicker, and then die.

Claudelle took the printout from the test and tried to fax it to Sylvie's office in Bordeaux, but Sylvie's fax machine wasn't working. Instead she called the office, and they had a quick conversation in French.

"It's not serious, I think," she said to me again. "Go home and relax, have a sleep, and then you will meet Sylvie at the hospital. At five o'clock, yes? But go home and lie down first."

I really don't blame Claudelle, though the day I asked the American nurse what they did when babies failed to respond was a very bad day for me. Let me be honest: it was a year to the day after the test with Claudelle, so it was already bad. I wish I hadn't asked.

Still, I don't blame Claudelle.

It's a strange business, turning those days into sentences, and then paragraphs. When I've thought of Claudelle since Pudding's death, it's been with sympathy: *she must feel terrible.* I've never wandered further down that road, wondered whether she feels culpable, whether she worries that she's the villain in our version of the story. I've never wondered whether it's terrible that we simply disappeared — because we did disappear, soon enough after that day we erased ourselves from that part of the world as completely as we could — or a relief. Maybe it's a relief. Maybe every day we stayed gone was a relief to her.

Or maybe it was just one of those sad things that happens when you're in the mostly joyful business of childbirth, and she never thinks of us at all.

We went out to lunch at an Indian restaurant close by. Edward's parents swore that really hot curries induced labor. In those days we drove miles and miles to find the curry houses of southwest France.

"Oh!" I said to Edward as we sat. "He just moved."

"Jolly good," he said.

I put my hand on top of my stomach and felt what I thought of as Pudding's rolling-over-in-bed move. "God, I feel better," I said. I exhaled. "All right. Well done, Pudding."

Later I found out that this was a Braxton Hicks contraction, my uterus puttering around, maybe getting ready for labor, maybe not. I found out, you see, because I continued to have them even after he was irrefutably dead.

We went back to Savary. I ate some cookies. At four we got in the car with my hospital bag—my clothes, Pudding's coming-home outfit, the books that Edward was going to read to me, the books I would read to myself. We always had great plans to read Dickens to each other, but we only ever got a chapter in at a time. Now it was *Great Expectations*—if we were only to get one chapter in, that was fine. We both know the book nearly by heart, and the first chapter is glorious, if, at this remove, a little overpopulated with dead children.

Again to Bordeaux in the rented car. We listened to *Round the Horne,* an old English radio program that Edward had bought me for Christmas. We had a CD of Mozart chosen especially for children for the three of us to listen to on the way back.

"I hate this," I said to Edward.

"I know," he answered.

"I *hate* this," I clarified.

He nodded.

Sylvie was not there when we arrived. We were taken to an examination room, where a very young male *sage-femme* — not very *sage,* not at all *femme* — shook our hands. He wore a pair of bright rubber clogs. I thought then that I would never forget what color they were, red or green or yellow, but I have no idea, I just remember that they were unusual.

He put the straps around my stomach and turned on the monitor. Nothing. He shifted them around.

He said, in French, I am going to go get my colleague. She is better at this than I am.

He disappeared and instead came back and brightly told us that we would go have a sonogram. Good, I thought. Enough messing around. Let's see the kid.

He led us into the hall and then out a side door. The sonographer's office was in a separate cottagey building, covered in lilacs, just outside the hospital. I had been there less than a week before, for a diagnostic scan, which led to a diagnostic X-ray: the doctor had thought there was something a little funny about my pelvis, an odd angle to my pubic bone. An X-ray after all! He had made it very clear: if the X-ray suggested that my pelvis was in fact a little funny, I would have to check into the hospital immediately for a C-section:

he wouldn't want to risk me going into labor. But my pubic
bone passed muster—I'd nervously told the technician I
was pregnant, just in case it wasn't glaringly obvious—and
so I'd gone home that day. "Thank God," I said to Edward
on the car ride home. "I'm really glad I'm not having an
impromptu caesarean." It felt like a narrow escape. Instead
we went home to wait some more.

You cannot.

So. It was a week later. The lilacs outside the entrance to
the sonography cottage were still in bloom. We were led by
the little male midwife past all the other people in the waiting room and into the two-room office. There was a desk
and two chairs in the front room, which is where you sat
and talked to the doctor when you weren't in a hurry. We
didn't stop. Last week's doctor was fortyish and spoke some
English. This week's was in his sixties, and didn't. I lay
down on the examining table. Edward sat in the husband's
chair in the corner of the room.

The doctor worked the paddle around my stomach. He
didn't pause. He searched and searched. If he stops I know
there's hope. But he doesn't stop.

I say, "Non?"

He doesn't look at me. He doesn't stop. But he says to the
screen, "Non."

I understand immediately and begin to sob.

Grief is a waterfall, and just like that I'm over it, no bar-
rel needed, I'm barrel-shaped.

Edward doesn't understand at first. "Comment?" he asks from his stool, and the male midwife says, "C'est fini." *It's finished*.

Here is exactly how I remember it.

The midwife threw himself into my arms. We embraced as the sonographer continued searching with his paddle, though what was he *looking* for, why wouldn't he leave me alone? (He was a diagnostician. He was looking for clues.) I submitted myself to the hug. I held still for the paddle. I tried to weep only from the chest up. Suddenly Edward had knocked aside the male midwife to take his place. He stroked my hair and told me that it was all right, it was all right, "Oh, sweetheart," he kept saying, "oh, sweetheart. It's going to be OK."

The midwife in his sorrow threw himself on Edward. Who knocked him aside again, saying, "Pas maintenant." *Not now*. My nice husband, who could not say simply, *Stop*, or *No*, or nothing at all. Poor midwife, who needed such comfort. Like anyone else in the profession he'd become a midwife for the babies, for the quotidian miracle of human reproduction. He was very young. This was probably his first death.

"Sweetheart," Edward kept saying. "It will be all right. We're going to be OK."

And I thought what a good man he was, that he was so understanding, because, and this made me weep harder, because I knew, I *knew*, that this was all my fault. My essential reaction was grief, but somehow the words that floated to the surface of my brain were: *people are going to be mad at me.*

Then the male midwife's head floated away from his body like a balloon and traveled up my torso. It said, "Ce n'est pas ta faute!"

It's not your fault.

It was my fault.

Edward turned to the doctor. "Et maintenant?" he asked.

The doctor shrugged, and spoke his second two words.

He said, "Le travail."

The work.

I would have to go through labor. I knew that already, the minute the doctor had shaken his head and said *Non*. The baby was dead, but he still had to be born. I knew this because my friend Wendy's sister had lost two late-term children to placenta previa. Before Wendy explained it, *stillbirth* to me was what happened in black-and-white engravings, in iron beds with nearby pitchers, and it was always a grim surprise. The baby was born. The attending physician shook his head. When Wendy explained it to me, I was shocked. I don't know how I supposed you got a late-term baby out.

"That's the worst thing in the world," I said to Wendy when she told me about her sister.

Now I understand. Of course it wasn't the worst thing in

the world. The worst thing in the world had already happened. He was dead. Everything else was easy.

I leaned on Edward. On the other side of the door was a waiting room full of pregnant women and their partners. On my side of the door, I thought, *Don't catch anyone's eye.*

I was not in shock. I was certainly not in denial. I was thinking quite clearly. I could remember what it was like to be pregnant and hopeful. That was minutes ago, though already in the remotest past. I had been shot out of a cannon since then, I was gone, but I knew: the women outside didn't deserve to see me, but they would. I had been hustled past them; I had disappeared and wailed; whenever a door opens into a waiting room, all eyes go to see who's behind it. In this case, me, the intact ruin. From the neck down I looked, like any heavily pregnant woman, like a monument to life. I knew where I was and what I was: bad luck for any pregnant woman to see. I was thirteen black cats. I was all the spilled salt in the world, a thousand smashed mirrors —

No. I was a dropped and dropping mirror. Look at me and see your reflection, for one clear instant before the disaster.

I unfocused my eyes and leaned harder on Edward and let him take me through the waiting room, past the lilacs, and back to the hospital proper.

The little midwife asked if I wanted a tranquilizer. Yes, please. He went running out of the room. We never saw him again.

. . .

A while later Sylvie, the delivering midwife, appeared in the room, and said —

Edward and I disagree about what she said. In a little while she would do something we couldn't forgive her for, but at that moment I still loved her. Even now, I don't hate her with the hot passion that Edward does, though I don't remember her with fondness. At any rate: I might in my confusion and sorrow have misheard her; Edward, in his sorrow and anger, might misremember. Everything, of course, is shrouded by our lack of fluency, since she spoke only French.

I thought she said, *Elizabeth, what has happened to your baby?*

Edward remembers, *Elizabeth, what have you done to your baby?*

I burst into tears.

You may add that detail into the description of the next five days approximately every four sentences. *I burst into tears. I got up. I pulled on my robe. I began to feel around in the dark. What do you need, what can I do? Edward asked me. I burst into tears.*

Et cetera.

She hugged me as I cried, and whatever the question was, she asked again, and I loved her. It was so early on, but here was another angle on my grief, and I was glad to get it. She had known Pudding in her way. She had listened to his heartbeat and pronounced it excellent; she had mapped its accelerations and decelerations. Now she said my name over and over, in the French way, Eeliza-*bett,* Eeliza-*bett,* and she seemed to understand that her hugging me made me cry harder, and that making me cry harder was something I'd be grateful for. The little male midwife had disappeared; the stern sonographer was back investigating the pregnancies of the lucky. Sylvie was here. She would help us get through all the very terrible things that came next.

Let's go get some air, she said, and we went outside.

The hospital we were at was small, one floor, with the aforementioned lilacs. It was decided that we would go to a different, larger hospital for *le travail.* Sylvie called the doctor who'd administered the sonogram the week before, and he drove over. Five days ago he'd spoken only a little English; suddenly, standing in the parking lot, he seemed fluent, sad but professional. We stood among the cars. He and Sylvie spoke in French and shrugged.

"You must see the baby," he advised us. It was the only medical advice he had left to give. "After he's born. You must see so you can understand, This is my baby, he is not a monster. This is very important."

We nodded. So did Sylvie. She said, "Très important. You muss."

"Yes," I said.

I didn't want to see the baby.

This was garden-variety fear, though I didn't understand that then. All I wanted was to be on the other side of what

was about to happen. Not just on the other side of the next
few days, the hospital stay, the terror of the delivery (a parody of the childbirth we'd been planning for and anxious
about), calling people (another parody of something we
were supposed to do; I was waiting until both of my parents would be home to call with the terrible news), getting
the hell out of France. The movers were due to pick up our
things and take them to England, and if I could have had
any wish granted at that moment — besides the obvious, of
course, that the sonograph was wrong, the pregnancy was
as uncomplicated as it had seemed to be all along, Pudding
was alive and would be born and squalling and confound-
ing us within hours — it would have been to be put under
anesthesia, the delivery to be done with. Then the movers
could pack me in a crate and send me to England. Maybe
by September it would be safe to take the crowbar to the
wood and part the excelsior and let me back into the
world.

Instead, we got in our car and followed Sylvie to the next
place.

The new hospital was a grim collection of urban buildings
set about with construction cranes. It was the main hospital
in Bordeaux, and the construction made it difficult to find
our way into the building. We went to an admitting room.
I sat on a table. We met a sympathetic young doctor, and
then a strange young anesthesiologist who spoke very good
English and seemed delighted to practice it despite the cir-

cumstances. I would take the epidural after all. A nurse came around with a clipboard, and we ran into the usual confusion over names. *McCracken* struck most French medical professionals as unthinkable — so many unwieldy consonants! — and besides, I was married, I said I was married, here was my husband, what was his name?

The nurse said, From now on, here, you are Mrs. Harvey.

I saw on my records a note from the morning, handwritten by Claudelle. It said that I was *très inquiète,* very worried, as though this were a medical diagnosis.

Sylvie came into the room, her cell phone ringing in her hand. She answered it.

"Ah, Claudelle," she said. "Le bébé est décédé. Oui. Oui. Le bébé est décédé."

Then she turned to me and said, It's Claudelle. You must talk to her.

I was in patient mode and nodded, though I was starting to realize something. I was done with Claudelle. Time on this planet actually ran in only one direction. No matter what, I could not travel backwards to a living baby and an ordinary birth, and I did not want to turn my head a fraction in the direction of the past. Not a second, not for anything. I was done with Claudelle, I was done with the Bordelaise roads I'd driven from the first hospital to this one. I did not want to retrace a thing.

This was a conversion moment for me. Twelve hours before, I'd barely believed in the future. I know that sounds crazy, especially for a pregnant woman. Don't get me wrong, I knew it existed. At the same time, the flat-earth part of my personality wanted to ask, Where's the proof? Of course the future kept arriving, of course it did, it arrived second by second, an assembly line of itself. But what I really believed in was the past, which is proven everywhere, and accessible: I'm a librarian, and I could show you where to look. The past is located in microfilm and bound volumes of magazines, in movies, memoirs, ephemera, granite, fluoroscopes in shoe stores; the career of Mamie Van Doren; the never mentioned first marriage and subsequent divorce of my cousin Elizabeth; speeding tickets; the daughters of Akhenaton; the invention of Silly Putty; trilobites. But the future? Let it come, let it age, let it be recorded, I'll get around to the future eventually.

That's what I thought until Pudding died, and then, at least for a while, I was like a sinner trembling on the edge of faith, demanding of the future: come, prove yourself, and I will renounce the past and everything I believe in.

In the exam room I did not yet have the courage of my convictions. I took the phone from Sylvie.

"Elizabeth, I am so sorry," Claudelle said. "Oh. I am so sorry. Please know my heart is with you."

"Yes," I said. "OK. Thank you."

Later I would wonder why Sylvie had made me talk to her. She did it with a kind of medical authority, and I dumbly accepted, thinking that she knew what I needed.

I don't think it did me a bit of good.

. . .

Edward and I clung to each other in the hallway of the Tripod Hospital, waiting for someone to take us to a room upstairs on the ward. The staff would see if they could find a cot for Edward. Otherwise he'd go to a hotel. A midwife passed by, a woman in her early fifties with short hair and a slightly daffy demeanor. She said, in French, Why do you look so sad? You're going to have a baby!

"Le bébé est décédé," Edward answered.

There's a certain French — gesture? moue? — that is ubiquitous and hard to translate. In answer to a question or piece of information, the French person fills his or her mouth with air and then puffs it out, eyebrows raised. It means, *It is difficult to say,* and it can be the answer to, *How do you drive to Lyon?* or *Do you have this in my size?* or, it turns out, *The baby is dead.*

Of course it all felt like an emergency to us, something to be taken care of immediately. Who would make a woman spend one more moment on this earth than is necessary with a dead child in her body? I thought I'd be induced instantly, I would deliver instantly, and then we could talk about leaving.

No. They would give me some medication to soften my cervix. The next day nothing would happen other than some blood tests to see if they could find an explanation. It's very important, the doctor on the ward explained. The day after that, they would induce, and *le travail* would commence when it commenced. We could only hope for the best.

The hospital room was no more picturesque for being French. They had found a folding cot for Edward, a miserable mid-1980s-ish polyester-sheeted appliance that meant he could sleep next to me, though at a considerable drop from the high hospital bed. There's a peculiar kind of loneliness, sleeping in a room near but not next to the person whose body you most require. He felt too far away. I'd wanted to trail my foot off the bed, dip it into his. Whenever I got up in the night to go to the bathroom — because there was still a weight pressing down on my bladder, the same as there had been the night before (before the baby had died) — Edward woke up at the slightest rustling of the sheets and took me there.

In the morning he folded the bed back up, and we asked the midwife if we could leave and go into Bordeaux. The morning's blood had already been taken. They had no more plans for me that day. She spoke to the doctor, and we were given a two-hour pass, as though I were a patient on a mental ward.

We left the car where it was and took the streetcar downtown and found one of Bordeaux's hidden backstreet plazas. As we turned the corner, a black cat suddenly ran in front of us.

"You're too late, mate," Edward told it.

We bought a pack of cigarettes without discussing it and sat down at a café, and I ordered an enormous glass of strong beer and lit up. We were in France. In the United States a heavily pregnant woman would be lynched for less, but here nobody seemed to notice.

The weather was horribly good.

That morning at 6:00 French time I had finally gotten hold of my parents. That is, my mother had answered the phone and I'd told her. It was not quite midnight in America. It was still the day before. Dark there, dawn in Bordeaux. My parents had been out at a party. I pictured my mother sitting on the edge of their bed. "Here," she said, "your father's just coming in, do you want—" Then she said in a certain voice, almost to herself, "I'll tell him." I was absurdly grateful that she'd made the decision for me. I could bear almost anything but breaking the news and wanted to do it as few times as possible.

(This is still true. There are friends, not close ones of course, who knew I was pregnant but did not hear what happened, and when they've written and said, "How's motherhood? Your son must be a year old by now!" I have simply never answered.)

At the café I called my parents again. My father answered, and when he heard my voice he said, "Oh, my darling, what can I say but that I love you with all of my heart."

I called my friend Ann. I could hear her excitement at my voice — she'd been waiting for her happy phone call —

and I told her my news and said that I needed a favor. Anything, she said, getting ahold of her tears. The sun at the café was quite bright.

I asked her to phone my friend Wendy and to split the calls to my other friends between them. I read aloud telephone numbers.

Why am I finding this harder to write about than anything?

There was no oxygen in the little plaza in Bordeaux. Edward and I both felt it. I could not look people in the eye, lest they smile and ask me about my baby.

"This was a mistake," said Edward. "We don't belong here."

Meaning, *Out in the world*. We'd escaped, but where could we go, with me in my condition?

Time had bent again. Time had developed a serious kink. Our old life — the one where we planned our existence around the son we were expecting — had ended, but our new life — the one where we tried to figure out how to live without him — couldn't start yet. We were stuck in a chronological bubble.

He was there, after all, still. He rode with us on the streetcar. He sat at the café table with us. He appeared in the shop windows we passed, though I didn't look to the side to see. We just pretended that he didn't.

Here's my question: was I pregnant then?

I was in the shape of a pregnant woman. I'm sure I

walked like one, though my arms floated away from the fact of my stomach (no rubbing, no resting, no thoughtless, fond tapping). Really, what was I? *Was* I pregnant? There should be a different word for it, for someone who hasn't yet delivered a dead child. Maybe there is and I don't know it, but I'm not about to ask.

My child had died. The next day I would see him for the first time. But until then, what was I? A figure common in old paintings and poetry. The bereaved carrying the remains of my beloved dead. Not out of bravery. Not out of devotion. Not out of hope that God had gotten it wrong and would change His mind.

Because I had to.

We went back to the hospital, where we could smoke on the park benches outside the building like the mental patients we were. Hard cases, not to be trusted with privileges.

A year later, when we spoke of the anniversary of Pudding's death, it was hard to know how to measure it. It felt like something biblical, though not out of the Testament I know anything about. He died, and then two days later he was born. Where was he in the meantime?

Since he died, I've never had a dream of him alive.

. . .

In the morning the ward midwife came to get us. We'd been awake for hours. I went down the hall first, to the showers, five tiny cabins on a narrow corridor. I barely fit. It was the first shower I'd taken since Pudding had died. I soaped myself without looking, dried myself with the sad French institutional towel, and put on the hospital gown.

What is there to say of the labor, the delivery? The midwives, one in her thirties and one in her early twenties, were sweet and attentive. The oddball anesthesiologist came back and gave a long lecture in English about epidurals, how they blocked both pain and the ability to sense temperature. He tested his work by running an ice cube down my leg. This epidural, he said, taking a seat next to my bed and crossing his legs in a jaunty manner, was self-administered. I would have a button to press for more relief. It still might run out, and I should say if it did. It did run out. They fed more medication into the machine, which fed into me. In that dry patch of no pain relief, I twisted Edward's hand and said in a panicked voice, "I don't want to do this, I don't want to do this!" but I gather plenty of women in labor say the same thing.

Edward and I had discussed it: I told him to leave the room for the actual delivery. It was a horrible thing to go through, and I wanted to spare him. That is, the watching seemed horrible to me. The delivery did not seem nearly so bad. Really, it felt like the last thing I could do for Pudding.

Edward had shouldered a great deal in the past few days, he had pushed his enormous pain aside to tend to me, and this seemed like one piece of pain I could keep him from. Pudding's death was something the two of us went through together. The delivery wasn't, couldn't be. In the end, it didn't even seem like something I went through. Those midwives in their French politeness called me Mrs. Harvey, *Madame Harvey*. They addressed me in the formal manner: *Poussez, Madame Harvey, très bien, Madame Harvey,* and that's who it was happening to, someone else, someone differently named, worthy of respect. The epidural did its job and I felt nothing and in the end it wasn't something Edward and I went through together and it wasn't something that I went through by myself. It was something that Pudding had to go through. We three women in the room did our best to help him but in the end he was alone.

They took him immediately from the room to clean him up and got Edward. He looked so sad, my poor husband. I don't know how long he'd been out of the room. Twenty minutes, I think. Everyone had told us that it was very important to see our child no matter what. Now we waited dutifully for Pudding. The nurses brought him in and set him on the delivery table, in front of where I sat cross-legged in my gown.

"He looks like an old man," Edward whispered, stroking his arm. A medium-sized baby, just over seven pounds. We touched him very tenderly. He wore a diaper and a knit yellow hat. The hair beneath the hat was dark, like mine. His cheeks were plump and his legs were skinny, and yellow, and undeniably dead. From the waist up he was rosy, and his lips were very, very red, very defined in his face. They were his father's lips.

We stroked him and told him we were sorry. Later Edward said, "I didn't know what it was I was feeling. Then I realized it was seeing someone and knowing immediately that you love him."

"We're ready," we told the midwives, and they took him away. My great regret is that I didn't pick him up.

For a long time when I looked at Edward, the first place my eyes stopped at was his mouth.

Faces famously fade from memory, and yet I swear I remember exactly what Pudding looked like. I'm glad I don't have a picture to contradict me. The lips and the rosiness were the result of blood and gravity. His lips were lovely because he was dead, and because he'd been upside down inside of me, and because he was dead.

All day long I wondered where Sylvie was. She had told me she would be there for the delivery. She finally showed up in the hospital room at five. The first thing she said was, Elizabeth, you were careful about what you ate, weren't you?

I was in bed, holding very still, but even so I froze. I said in my bad French, I thought I was, but maybe . . .

That's not it, said Edward.

She got a frightened look on her face and began to pat my frozen arms. Your baby, she said in French, your poor baby. *She's trying to make me cry,* I thought, and I still think that's what she was doing: she was worried that we blamed her, and so she tried to push the blame off onto me, and then she realized it was perhaps not the right time for such a transfer and tried to distract us from what she'd just said. She patted my arms harder. It's very sad, she said.

I wanted her to leave, but I could not ask, because of course this was all my fault. I still believed that, a conviction so awful and unshakable that I didn't say it aloud. If I'd said it to Edward, he would have tried to dissuade me, and my belief was an inoperable cancer, dangerous where it was but more dangerous to move. I could not put my finger on what I had done wrong. Eaten something. Failed to eat something. Rested too much or exercised too much. Got pregnant too old. Was smug. He died inside of me: Of course it was my fault. It happened on my watch.

I think, said Edward in a firm voice, Elizabeth would like it if you'd leave now. At the time it seemed like an astonishing piece of mind reading. Sylvie nodded and got up. Call me before you leave Bordeaux, she said, but we never did.

The midwife on the ward the next day was the kindest of all of them, in her forties, with dark hair gathered back and a careworn face. She gave me a sponge bath, and then she said, How are you?

Not good, I said.

But how, she asked me seriously, is your morale?

I smiled. I said, still smiling, not good. Not terrible but not good.

Of all the people who attended to me over those days, she was the only one who seemed to know that a sad thing had happened.

As she left I said, You're very kind.

She shrugged. Then she said, "C'est normal," it's normal, which means, of course, Who wouldn't be kind to you? But she said it in a voice that suggested that she knew: it wasn't normal after all.

I have mostly forgiven myself, and on good days I can
say, What else could I have done?

I find myself thankful for large and small things, in the
way of people who've lost two limbs and are glad not to
have lost four. Labor and delivery took four hours altogether; that was a mercy. They gave me medication that
prevented my milk from coming in, which worked: that,
too. We were thankful for the midwives who'd delivered
Pudding. The young one said, *À bientôt,* when she left, *See
you soon.* We were thankful that we could leave France,
thankful that we could live near the sea for a few months,
extraordinarily thankful that I got pregnant again so soon,
and that the pregnancy held. I am not sure what sort of
person I would be if that hadn't happened.

Even now I feel a scalding, pleasureless relief that I
pressed Claudelle to see me that morning. I wish I had
pressed her more; I wish I had alarmed her into sending
me immediately to the hospital — the one in Bordeaux, or

the more terrifying one five minutes away from her office. But in the absence of that, I am relieved that when she said, Come at five, I'd said no. If I'd gone at five, Pudding would have been dead already. I wouldn't have known when it had happened, and I don't know how I would have gone forward in the world.

A year and three days after the morning I checked out of the hospital, Edward and I woke up in our second rented house in Saratoga Springs, an enormous Victorian we'd moved to a month before. The grubby rental house was around the corner. We might have stayed, but the owners decided to put it on the market, and so we ended up a block away, in a place that, it would turn out, had bats. We ate a small breakfast and wondered what the day would be like. We still weren't people who could say under such circumstances, "By this time tomorrow, we'll have a baby!"

I got dressed in a pair of stretchy black pants and a stretchy black top and put on lipstick and asked Edward to take my photograph: I hadn't posed for a single picture for all of this pregnancy. I stood on the porch and smiled. It was a lovely spring day. Then we walked to the hospital.

Nurses are like anyone else when it comes to small talk, and while they went about their work they asked the usual questions. Boy or girl? Have you picked out a name? Are you wearing *lipstick*? To deliver a baby? At one point I had nurses on both arms looking for a likely vein for the IV. "You have very slender veins," said one, pulling out a failed line.

"Shall we call for Marilyn?" another asked.

No, I thought, I wouldn't name a baby Marilyn.

The mention of Marilyn, legendarily good at IVs, roused the competitive spirit of the first nurse. "Let me try again," she said, and moved up my arm. This time when she failed she left behind an enormous amethyst bruise.

"Shall we call for anesthesia?" said the nurse who'd suggested calling for Marilyn, and I thought dreamily, *Anesthesia. That's a nice name.*

The anesthesiologist came to put in the IV. He thought we looked familiar, and realized he'd seen us the night before at the DMV. That was somehow unnerving.

The nurse started the Pitocin drip. Dr. Knoeller came by.

"What are you thinking for names?" she asked.

We said we weren't sure.

"Well," she said, "I have a spare boy's name, if it's a boy."

We stared at her, our hearts full of love, sure that this would be the best boy's name ever.

"Lance," she said.

Which immediately struck me as an unfortunate name for the son of a doctor.

. . .

Even happy labor stories can be excruciating in their details. The Pitocin drip went in at 9:30 a.m. I was hooked up to a fetal heart rate monitor and a contraction monitor, the same sorts I'd been on twice a week at the practice. After several hours I asked the young nurse, "Am I having any contractions yet?"

" 'Bout every two to three minutes," she said. I hadn't felt a thing.

I was glad that Edward hadn't been in the room for Pudding's delivery: now, when I looked up at him from the delivery table it would be new, and when he told me we were almost there it would be new, it would be what I'd expected, and wholly unfamiliar. He opened a book to read to me. *David Copperfield* this time, which begins with a hair-raising birth. "Keep going," I told him, admiring the great girth of the rest of the account of that baby's life.

Dr. Knoeller stripped my membranes at 5:00. At 6:00 I asked for an epidural. At 7:36—

I'm skipping some details: the baby's heart began to decelerate during contractions. Dr. Knoeller came in to check me and was surprised to see that I was fully dilated. The baby's heartbeat continued to decelerate during contractions. I became aware of the decelerations, even though I couldn't feel the contractions: I could hear the beeping monitor. I started to watch the clock on the wall and could see that sometimes the heartbeats were in step with the second hand: sixty beats a minute, good for a grown-up but bad for a baby. My old fetish, the heartbeat. This monitor, threaded up me and onto the baby's head, had a cold science-fiction beep. It was time to push, but it was hard when the effort came at the same time the heartbeat slowed: I tried to concentrate on my work, *the work,* but I couldn't with that soundtrack. They put an oxygen mask on me so the baby would get more oxygen. Dr. Knoeller and the nurses told me that I was doing wonderfully, I was almost there. Edward was stroking my forehead and saying the same thing. Maybe they were lying. I suspected that they were. One of the nurses said to Dr. Knoeller — I didn't hear her, thank God; Edward told me later — that the umbilical cord was wrapped around the baby's neck. They told me to rest, and the heartbeat sped up. They told me to push and it slowed down again.

Then the heartbeat stopped.

Then my heart broke.

And then — look, we're at 7:36 again — there was suddenly a toasty warm, hollering, wet baby on my chest, and Edward and I were laughing, and laughing, and laughing. He was actual! An actual baby, pulled from the dream of my body into the shocking wakefulness of earthly life. Maybe he thought the same of us: all that warmth, those dim voices, the love taps, the questions — I thought I'd made you up.

"It's a little boy!" said Edward.

"Did you see?" said Dr. Knoeller.

"A little boy!" Edward told her.

He was small and skinny, six pounds and change, twenty inches long.

When Dr. Knoeller left she kissed us, and hugged us, and said, "Well, I don't know about you, but I'm up for doing this again."

Even so, we didn't name him Lance.

In the hospital room, we tried out names. We hadn't seriously played at this game since before Pudding was born. He looked absolutely unlike a Moses. He looked, in fact, like Edward, fair-haired and big-eyed and worried. "Isn't he just like his father!" the nurses kept saying admiringly, as though this was a great trick the three of us had pulled off. Oh, he was beautiful, entirely himself.

We discussed Barnaby, Felix, Thomas, and Arthur. "The boy who wasn't Mabel," Lib said, when Edward called. We understood that Oscar was out: we were pretty sure that's what Pudding's name would have been, had he lived. This baby deserved a name of his own. But what would suit him?

"Barnaby Harvey," I kept saying, and Edward shook his head.

"I've always loved the name Thomas," he kept saying, and I shook my head.

"August," he said, reading from the book of baby names I'd bought fifteen years before for fictional characters. "We could call him Augie, or Gus. Gus, I think."

"Sidney," I said.

"Maybe. Sidney. Sid. It's a no-nonsense, tough name, Sid. Your mate down at the pub."

The Sid I knew best was the husband of the president of my grandmother's temple sisterhood, a sweet uxorious pharmacist. "Maybe not," I said.

"Gus, then," said Edward. "I think Gus."

That night, when Edward went home to get some sleep, I tried it out. The baby was in his plastic hospital bassinet, swaddled into a neat and uncanny little package. I could see only his head in its mint green cap. "Hello, Gus," I said. "Hello, Gussie. Hello, Gusling. Hello, Gosling."

Sometime around 2:00 a.m., it had settled in my mind, and so I told the baby the story of his older brother. I really did: this isn't literary fancifulness. He was a little, little baby, and I told him the story out loud, not knowing when we might tell him again: I wanted him to know how glad we were to see him, and how sad we were that he'd never know his older brother.

"I think your name is Gus," I told him, and of course now I can't imagine why we thought his name could ever be anything else.

Later that week, after we'd come home from the hospital, the baby clothes arrived from England. We'd thrown away anything really difficult, or burned it behind Savary. Still, for a while I just stood and looked at open boxes. Then I took out a piece of clothing, a pair of blue striped pull-on pants, and without thinking I brought them to my face and breathed in.

Of course they wouldn't smell like him. He died in Bordeaux. What sentimental perfume did I think I'd find on them anyhow, what essence of Puddingness?

And yet they did smell of him. That is, they smelled of the sweet milky French baby soap we'd bought in Duras. Savary had a washing machine but not a dryer, and we'd washed everything and then hung it to dry on the lines on the south side of the terrace. Those lines were way over my head — I had to stand on tiptoe and grab them down — and the clothes were very small and sweet as they dried. So the pants and everything in the box *did* smell like Pudding, that is, they smelled of our last optimistic days at the house as we did the last bits of nest feathering before we brought our son home. I'd forgotten the smell (as you do of a lost person), but now here it was, three boxes full.

I found that my heart could take it, and I started to unpack. At first every now and then I'd get a flutter and think, *I remember when I bought this for him,* and then I'd look at the label inside — Baby Gap or Old Navy or Carter's — and would realize it was a hand-me-down from the little American boy in Cambridge. A few articles of clothing felt very sad to me, items of clothing so charming and peculiar that they'd been part of the story we'd told ourselves, "Our Life with Pudding": some particularly stylish clothing that my friend Monica had sent to us, the tiny pair of plaid wool knee pants that I'd bought in Bergerac for two euros. We'd often looked at this clothing when I'd been pregnant, and hurriedly packed it up when we'd returned from the hospital. We put away the sweaters that Edward's mother had made, because they had been made particularly for Pudding. They're his, and his alone.

But even the most fraught of the other clothing feels fine now. Of course it reminds us of Pudding, but when have we ever forgotten? Indeed, we want to remember him, and it doesn't feel strange or grim to put Gus into a pair of pants that we'd imagined Pudding wearing. People wear clothing that belonged to their dead all the time: a father's Irish sweater, a grandfather's felt hat, a grandmother's Peter Pan–collared shirt. I can look at those plaid pants and remember, for once, not Pudding's death, but the pleasure I took in finding them for sale, for so cheap, how funny I thought those plaid pants would look on a little boy.

And now I'm thinking of that Florida lady again, the one who wanted a book about the lighter side of a child's death, and I know: all she wanted was permission to remember her child with pleasure instead of grief. To remember that he was dead, but to remember him without pain: he's dead but of course she still loves him, and that love isn't morbid or bloodstained or unsightly, it doesn't need to be shoved away.

It isn't so much to ask.

When I was pregnant with Gus, toward the end especially, there was nothing in my life that was not bittersweet. Every piece of hope was tinged with sadness; every moment of relief was lit on the edges with worry. But now that Gus is Stateside, my love for him is just plain love, just plain sweet. He's such a beautiful funny thing, entirely himself, innocent of history. "It's you!" I say to him. "All that time, it was you! Who'd 'a thunk it?"

Of course he doesn't erase his older brother's death. He's a little baby: we'd never ask him to do such a job. Monkeying in the ways of the dead is for reincarnated llamas, or infant queens, not our child. His job is to be Gus. In this he more than pulls his weight.

He has cured me, mostly, of blame and what might have been, all of that fairy-tale bargaining: *what would you do differently* and *what if*. I know my fairy tales. Those bargains are disastrous: you ask for what you want, and then your words get twisted. Terrible things happen. It's never so easy as a wish. Sometimes I think I'm ready. Whoever shows up, some cerulean fairy, some adenoidal troll, the magic goddamn galoshes, I will have a knife to its neck in a second. I will say: All my children, healthy, normal, nothing else. No? You won't do it? Then leave me alone.

But generally my door is barred to all bargaining apparitions. Sometimes I look at Gus, and it all feels very familiar. Not *him*. He was a skinny just-born, with cheekbones and an incensed cry: he looked like an old man who'd been outfitted with hands and feet a size too big and he wanted to know to which knucklehead he should address his complaint. Now he is fat and looks like a retired advertising executive. He is gorgeous and inscrutable. I tell you, I've never seen his like.

But taking care of him, changing him, nursing him, I felt as though I'd done it before, as though it were true: time did split in half, and in some back alley of the universe I took care of Pudding, when he was a tiny baby, and *this* reminds me of *that*. There's a strange museum/gift shop/ antique store/tourist trap in Schuylerville, New York, the next town over. In front is a reconstruction of colonial Fort George done in wood cutouts—a soldier in stocks, Revolutionary soldiers in profile, all cut with a jigsaw and painted in bright colors. In front is a sign that says: *An exact replica of a figment of my imagination,* and that is what this life feels like some days. It's a happy life, but someone is missing. It's a happy life, *and* someone is missing.

It's a happy life—

—Saratoga Springs, New York
June 2007

Acknowledgments

Henry Dunow, my friend and agent, read the manuscript in its earliest state, and was — as he has been for the nearly twenty years I have known him — so smart and kind I cannot describe it, nor adequately thank him for it.

I also want to thank Paul Lisicky, whose reading made all the difference to me (and whose friendship likewise does); Ann Patchett, of course and as usual; Wendy Owen; and Betsy Lerner.

More thanks to: Reagan Arthur, Oliver Haslegrave, Jayne Yaffe Kamp, and everyone at Little, Brown.

I hope my gratitude for everything else and to everyone else is legible in the pages of this book.